THE

THE DEMI-GODS

BY

JAMES STEPHENS

AUTHOR OF
The Charwoman's Daughter, The Hill of Vision,
The Crock of Gold, etc.

WITH AN INTRODUCTION BY
AUGUSTINE MARTIN

BUTLER SIMS PUBLISHING LTD
DUBLIN

First published 1914 by Macmillan and Company Ltd
This edition published 1982 by
Butler Sims Publishing Ltd, 24 Anglesea St, Dublin 2, Ireland

British Library Cataloguing in Publication Data
Stephens, James
The Demi-Gods
I. Title
823′. 912(F)   PR6037.T4

ISBN 0–946049–02–5

Filmset in Monophoto Times by
Northumberland Press Ltd, Gateshead
Printed and bound in Great Britain by
Richard Clay (The Chaucer Press) Ltd, Bungay, Suffolk

CONTENTS

BOOK I
PATSY MAC CANN

15

BOOK II
EILEEN NI COOLEY

63

BOOK III
BRIEN O'BRIEN

95

BOOK IV
MARY MAC CANN

141

INTRODUCTION

WHEN James Stephens published *The Demi-Gods* in 1914 he was at the zenith of his career as a writer. It was his fourth book of fiction in two years. In 1912 he had had remarkable success with his novel of the Dublin slums *The Charwoman's Daughter* and his Celtic fantasy *The Crock of Gold*. The following year saw the publication of his first short story collection *Here Are Ladies*. All three books were acclaimed on both sides of the Atlantic and Stephens was seen by many as the most promising young writer on the Irish scene. His exact contemporary, later his friend, James Joyce was still struggling with recalcitrant publishers to have *Dubliners* brought out. It appeared in the same year as *The Demi-Gods*. Thereafter Joyce was to dominate the scene, especially among the intellectuals and in academe. But though Stephens was little cultivated by the clerisy he never failed with the reading public. *The Crock of Gold* has never been out of print, and at this moment the short stories, *The Charwoman's Daughter* and *Irish Fairy Tales* are available from Irish publishers. The present issue of *The Demi-Gods* is a most welcome addition to the canon. Though it has not had the critical or commercial success of *The Crock* it is arguably the funniest and most ingenious of his prose fantasies.

The impression left on the memory by a reading of *The Demi-Gods* is primarily that of the tinkers—Patsy Mac Cann and his daughter Mary, his fiery lover Eileen Ni Cooley, and their strange wanderings round the boreens of Ireland in the company of three angels recently alighted on the orb. One then recalls strange interstellar shenanigans: a quarrel in

7

heaven about a threepenny piece resulting in the expulsion of the Seraph Cuculain and his enemy Brien O'Brien who land naked on the Donnybrook Road and strip the Mac Canns of their clothes. Then there is the evangelical tramp Billy the Music who had once been an avaricious farmer until the curse of Midas struck him—through the agency of Cuchulain—and he took to the roads with his concertina. Other memories are even more bizarre—several accounts of creation, conversations between humans and donkeys, between an angel and a spider, a magician—weirdly prophetic of *Star Wars*—struggling to thwart the universe as it cranks itself into a new phase of spiritual evolution. One can forgive those critics—most recently Harmon and McHugh in their fine *History of Anglo-Irish Literature*— who find the narrative 'diffuse', though one inclines to the view of Benedict Kiely who perceives a design in it all—'the little heedless roads that the angels and tinkers travelled together led back to where the celestial garments ... had been hidden so that they could for a time appear like men in the world of men.'

Indeed the tinkers are so brilliantly characterised, and their adventures so vivid that there is a temptation to resent any intrusion, however heavenly, into their world. Yet if we accept that nothing in the book is an intrusion, that nothing is a digression, that it is one of the most cunningly plotted narrative structures in Irish fiction, our enjoyment will increase dramatically. *The Demi-Gods*, in its own comic idiom, is nothing less than Stephen's attempt to clarify the ways of god to men, an enterprise he persisted in through most of his mystical and visionary poetry, notably *The Hill of Vision* published too in that *'annus mirabilis'* of 1912.

The over-arching plot of the book involves two love stories, that of the young angel Art and Mary Mac Cann, and that of the two tinkers Patsy Mac Cann and Eileen Ni

Cooley. Both stories lead to marriage in the novel's fourth and last book, thus fulfilling the form of the romantic comedy. The union of an angel and a mortal is nothing new in Stephens: *The Crock of Gold* ended with the marriage of the god Angus Og with Caitilin, the farmer's daughter. But its symbolic implications cannot be ignored, any more than the celestial forces that conspire at the reconciliation of those ferocious lovers, Patsy and Eileen. As the fable proceeds we discover that each of the three angels has an earthly counterpart. Finaun is paired with Eileen, Caeltia with Patsy, and Art with Mary. In Christian terms the three visitors can be seen as guardian angels, in Hermetic terms they vindicate the doctrine that all things on earth are copies of heavenly things. When Finaun and Caeltia take off for heaven at the end they have wrought the reconciliation of Patsy and Eileen—hitherto warring principles. Art remains behind with Mary to seal the bargain.

Behind the story lies Stephen's belief, derived from Blake and the Theosophists, that the world consists of opposing forces—good/evil, night/day, man/woman, spirit/matter, love/hate. Thus in Book II, Chapter XVI Finaun's account of creation describes an archetypal struggle between two principles called Finaun and Caeltia Mac Dea whose sexes constantly interchange and who are destined to 'pursue each other with a hate that is slowly changing into love.' Eileen understands and likes the story, but Patsy unfortunately has been asleep. He will have to discover its application through the experience of the book's action. This he does; and he learns other lessons as well.

One of these lessons has to do with greed, money, property and power. It centres mostly on the tale of Billy the Music. When this reformed predator tells his story of exploitation the earthly and the celestial again come together. Cuchulain and Brien O'Brien arrive at his farm and the former has strange tidings:

9

'I'm your Higher Self,' said he, 'and every rotten business you do down here does be vibrating against me up there ... You're a miser and a thief, and you got me thrown out of heaven because of the way you loved money ... You made a thief out of me in a place where it's no fun to be a robber, and here am I wandering the dirty world on the head of your unrighteous ways.'

At this point Patsy interpolates the story of being stripped on the Donnybrook Road, and immediately afterwards Caeltia fills in the extra-terrestrial adventures of O'Brien and Cuchulain. O'Brien's misfortunes had their root in greed. At his funeral a neighbour had slipped a threepenny piece into his daughter's hand and she, in obedience to a lifetime of schooling, had slipped it in turn into her father's hand: 'The hand had never refused money when it was alive, it did not reject it either when it was dead.' It was when O'Brien subsequently dropped it on the floor of heaven and Cuchulain picked it up that their cosmic tribulations began. All of which enforces Stephens's belief that the traffic between this world and the next is not all one way.

Patsy Mac Cann is a magnificent characterisation. Having welcomed the angels to his camp he then determines to steal away on them in the night—'we don't know who them fellows are at all, and what would the priest say if he heard we were stravaiging the country with three big, buck-angels, and they full of tricks maybe?' When Mary—who is falling in love with Art—insists on adopting them she appeals to Mac Cann's greedy instincts, pointing out their gold rings. Then there stirs in his mind a more momentous instinct:

In his soul the Ancient Patriarch was alive and ambitious for leadership. Had his wife given him more children he would have formed them and their wives and children into a band, and the affairs of this little world would have

10

been directed by him with pride and pleasure ... he would have taken to the road, like a prince of old, with his tail, and he would have undertaken such raids and forays that his name and fame would ring through the underworld like the note of a trumpet.

Patsy's two temptations have to do with love and property. He fails in his love for Eileen as long as he succumbs to violent jealousy. He is no match for his rival, that shambling tramp whom Stephens catches in one of his most memorable word pictures: 'Nothing of comeliness remained to him but his eyes, which were timid and tender as those of a fawn, and his hands which had never done anything but fumble with women.' He sins against the daily, freebooting code of vagrancy when he steals and sells the angels' rings and garments. When Caeltia persuades him to throw away his ill-gotten gold at the end he allows one coin to slip to the bottom of his pocket. When he confesses this to Caoilte he is allowed to keep it. '"I'll keep it," said he earnestly, "and I'll spend it"'. Thus he returns to the hunter's life that had hitherto kept him free from the tyranny of an acquisitive society.

To say that the book is subversive is to put things mildly. Among the issues Mac Cann tries to explain to the angels is the social structure which he only vaguely comprehends as he has always lived outside it. But he recalls a conversation he once had with a tramp who held the view that 'the folk at the top do grab all the food in the world, and that then they make every person work for them, and that when you've done a certain amount of work they give you just enough money to buy just enough food to go on working for them.'

When Billy the Music describes how he exploited his employees before his conversion he declares: 'I found that there was a world outside my world, and that it was truly robbing me, and what's more, it had thought hard for

11

generations about the best way of doing it.' Mac Cann swears that he would have broken Billy's teeth with a spade if he had been one of his workers:

'If you were one of my men,' the other replied mildly ...
'you would have crawled round me with your hat in your hand and your eyes turned up like a duck's, and you'd have said, "Yes sir" and "No sir" like all the other men I welted the stuffing out of with my two fists, and broke the spirits of with labour and hunger. Don't be talking now, for you're an ignorant man in these things, although you did manage to steal a clocking hen off me the day I was busy.'
'And a pair of good boots,' said Patsy triumphantly.

Stephens had long suffered at the hands of society when he had been a wage-slave in a law office. His hatred of the capitalist system is in evidence through his early poems and reaches its most concentrated expression in his great story 'Hunger'. In *The Demi-Gods* it loses little of its force from being encased in a sheath of comedy.

This comic structure with its elaborately interconnected plots and its shifting angles of narration enables the author to present us with a world view, rather than a strictly local or social view. At one moment we are in the outer spaces of the theosophist heaven, at another we are caught up in petty larceny just inside the pearly gates, at another we are listening to a spider explaining the micro-economics of his life-style to a sympathetic angel:

'Are the times bad with you now, or are they middling?'
'Not so bad, glory be to God! The flies do wander through the holes, and when they come from the light outside to the darkness in here, sir, we catch them on the wall, and we crunch their bones.'
'Do they like that?'

'They do not sir, but we do. The lad with the stout, hairy legs down there beside your elbow, caught a blue-bottle yesterday; there was eating on that fellow I tell you, and he's not all eaten yet, but that spider is always lucky, barring the day he caught a wasp.'

'That was a thing he didn't like?'

'Don't mention it to him, sir, he doesn't care to talk about it.'

'What way are you going to fasten up your rope?' asked Art.

'I'll put a spit on the end of it, and then I'll thump it with my head to make it stick.'

'Well, good luck to yourself.'

'Good luck to your honour.'

Such winsome moments act in resonant counterpoint to the kind of cosmic crisis that Art describes at the end of Book III when he acts as one of the regent Seven as the Army of the Voice tries to project the universe into a new stage of psychic development. Here he finds himself hindered by the troglodite O'Brien who has surrounded himself by cab-balistic symbols in order to thwart the enterprise. When Stephens wrote his book he was in Paris where the war of the Theosophists and the cabbalistic devotees of the Golden Dawn was still alive. O'Brien is probably based on Yeats's associate, the 'great magician' McGregor Mathers—or even more plausibly on his 'unspeakable' colleague the *Great Beast*, Aleister Crowley. The purer Theosophists—natural allies of soulful spiders—disapproved of magic. O'Brien fancied himself as 'a great magician ... and a great humourist'. According to Finaun the two conditions are incompatible because 'Humour is the health of the mind.'

Humour is the master principle of *The Demi-Gods*. A reading of Madame Blavatsky's *Secret Doctrine*, Yeats's *Autobiographies* or Mathers's *Kabbala Unveiled* might help a

13

little with the more esoteric passages of Stephens's fantasy, but is certainly not necessary. The fact is that though Stephens was deeply absorbed in mystical doctrines he always treated them in a spirit of irreverence, humour, if not downright parody in his prose fictions. I have pointed out elsewhere that *The Crock of Gold* embodies a gentle mockery of Yeatsean apocalypse and of A.E.'s belief in the return of the old gods to Ireland. It contains muted parodies of Colum and Synge just as *The Charwoman's Daughter* offers comic pen pictures of A.E., John B. Yeats and George Moore. Like Moore's *Hail and Farewell* Stephens's fantasies vividly reflect the mental and spiritual climate of a literary movement which was alive with doctrinal eccentricity. And while some of the doctrines have lost their appeal they enhance rather than diminish the fictional performance, which preserves them like flies within the glow of its amber.

Finally *The Demi-Gods* shares with *The Crock of Gold* a seminal role in the development of experimental prose fiction in Ireland, the tradition that includes Eimar O'Duffy, Samuel Becket, Flann O'Brien, Mervyn Wall, Tom McIntyre and Joyce himself. This tradition can express itself through the idyll, as in Bryan McMahon's *Children of the Rainbow*, through the re-shaping of folk material as in Benedict Kiely's *Cards of the Gambler*, through the burlesque of myth as in O'Duffy's King Goshawk or Joyce's Cyclops. It would be hard to conceive of Colum's *King of Ireland's Son* or Clarke's medieval romances without the pioneering influence of Stephens. Yet it is not for what it did, but for what it is, that we re-read *The Demi-Gods*. I envy the reader who is now opening it for the first time.

AUGUSTINE MARTIN

BOOK I
PATSY MAC CANN

CHAPTER I

'WILL you leave that donkey alone?' said Patsy Mac Cann to his daughter. 'I never heard the like of it,' he continued testily. 'I tell you the way you do be going on with the ass is enough to make a Christian man swear, so it is.'

'You let me be,' she replied. 'If I was doing hurt or harm to you I wouldn't mind, and if I am fond of the ass itself what does it matter to anybody?'

'It's this way, that I don't like to see a woman kissing an ass on the snout, it's not natural nor proper.'

'A lot you know about natural and proper. Let you leave me alone now; and, besides that, doesn't the ass like it?'

'That's not a reason; sure it doesn't matter in the world what an ass likes or dislikes, and, anyhow, an ass doesn't like anything except carrots and turnips.'

'This one does,' said she stoutly.

'And a body might be kissing an ass until the black day of doom and he wouldn't mind it.'

'This one minds.'

'Kissing an old ass!'

'One has to be kissing something.'

'Let you kiss me then and get done with it,' said he.

She regarded him in amazement.

'What would I kiss you for? Sure you're my father, and aren't you as old as the hills?'

'Well, well, you're full of fun, and that's what I say. Take the winkers off that donkey's face, and let him get a bit to eat; there's grass enough, God knows, and it's good grass.'

Mary busied herself with the winkers and the bit while her father continued:

'What I wish is this, that Christian people were able to eat grass like the beasts, and then there wouldn't be any more trouble in the world. Are you listening to me, Mary, or are you listening to the donkey?'

'It's you I'm listening to.'

'I say this, that if every person had enough to eat there'd be no more trouble in the world and we could fight our fill. What have you got in the basket?'

'I've the loaf that I bought in the shop at Knockbeg, and the half loaf that you took out of the woman's window—it's fresher than the other one.'

'I was guided,' said her father. 'We'll eat that one first the way no person can claim it. What else have you got?'

'I've the white turnip that I found in a field.'

'There's great nourishment in turnips; the cattle do get fat on them in winter.'

'And I've the two handfuls of potatoes that you gathered at the bend of the road.'

'Roast themselves in the embers, for that's the only road to cook a potato. What way are we going to eat to-night?'

'We'll eat the turnip first, and then we'll eat the bread, and after that we'll eat the potatoes.'

'And fine they'll taste. I'll cut the turnip for you with the sailorman's jack-knife.'

The day had drawn to its close. The stars had not yet come, nor the moon. Far to the west a red cloud poised on the horizon like a great whale and, moment by moment, it paled and faded until it was no more than a pink flush. On high, clouds of pearl and snow piled and fell and sailed away on easy voyages. It was the twilight—a twilight of such quietude that one could hear the soft voice of the world as it whispered through leaf and twig. There was no breeze to swing the branches of the trees or to creep among the rank grasses and set them dancing, and yet everywhere there was

18

unceasing movement and a sound that never ceased. About them, for mile upon mile, there was no habitation of man; there was no movement anywhere except when a bird dipped and soared in a hasty flight homewards, or when a beetle went slugging by like a tired bullet.

Mary had unharnessed the ass and bade him, with an affectionate kiss, to eat his fill. The donkey stood for a moment with his ears and tail hanging down, then he lifted both his ears and his tail, slung up his ragged head, bared his solid teeth, and brayed furiously for two minutes. That accomplished, he trotted briskly a few paces, bent to the grass, and began to eat so eagerly that one would think eating was more of a novelty to him than it could be to an ass of his years.

'The sound of that beast's voice does get on my nerves,' said Patsy.

'He has a powerful voice, sure enough, God bless him! Sit down there by the hedge and light the fire while I'm getting the things ready; the night will be on us in a few minutes and it will be a cold night.'

While she moved busily from the cart to the hedge her father employed himself lighting a fire of turf in a wrinkled bucket. When this was under way he pulled out a pipe, black as a coal, and off which half the shank was broken, and this he put into his mouth. At the moment he seemed to be sunken in thought, his eyes to the grass and his feet planted, and it was in a musing voice that he spoke:

'Do you know what I'd do, Mary, if I had a bottle of porter beside me in this field?'

'I do well,' she replied; 'you'd drink it.'

'I would so, but before I'd drink it I'd put the end of this pipe into it, for it's newly cracked, and it sticks to my lips in a way that would anger a man wanting a smoke, and if I could stick it into the porter it would be cured. I don't suppose, now, that you have a sup of porter in the cart!'

19

'I have not.'

'Because if you had a small sup I'd be able to get a smoke this night, as well as a drink.'

'You're full of fun,' said she sourly.

'I saw a bottle in your hand a while back,' he continued musingly, 'and it looked like a weighty bottle.'

'It's full to the neck with spring water.'

'Ah!' said her father, and he regarded that distant horizon whereon the pink cloud was now scarcely visible as a pinkness and was no longer the shape of a great whale.

After a moment he continued in a careless voice:

'You might hand me the bottle of spring water, alanna, till I wet my lips with it. It's a great thing for the thirst, I'm told, and it's healthy beside that.'

'I'm keeping that sup of water to make the tea when we'd be wanting it.'

'Well, I'll only take a drop out of it, and I won't lose the cork.'

'You can get it yourself then,' said Mary, 'for I've plenty to do, and you haven't.'

Her father, rolling his tough chin with his fingers, went to the cart. He found the bottle, lifted the cork, smelt it, tasted:

'It is spring water indeed,' said he, and he thumped the cork back again with some irritation and replaced the bottle in the cart.

'I thought you wanted a drink,' said his daughter mildly.

'So I do,' he replied, 'but I can't stand the little creatures that do be wriggling about in spring water. I wouldn't like to be swallowing them unknown. Ah! them things don't be in barrels that you buy in a shop, and that's a fact.'

She was preparing the potatoes when a remark from her father caused her to pause.

'What is it?' said she.

'It's a bird. I saw it for a second against a white piece of a cloud, and I give you my word that it's as big as a haystack.

There it is again,' he continued excitedly; 'there's three of them.'

For a few minutes they followed the flight of these amazing birds, but the twilight had almost entirely departed and darkness was brooding over the land. They did not see them any more.

CHAPTER II

AND yet it was but a short distance from where they camped that the angels first put foot to earth.

It is useless to question what turmoil of wind or vagary of wing brought them to this desert hill instead of to a place more worthy of their grandeur, for, indeed, they were gorgeously apparelled in silken robes of scarlet and gold and purple; upon their heads were crowns high in form and of curious, intricate workmanship, and their wings, stretching ten feet on either side, were of many and shining colours.

Enough that here they did land, and in this silence and darkness they stood for a few moments looking about them.

Then one spoke:

'Art,' said he, 'we were too busy coming down to look about us carefully; spring up again a little way, and see if there is any house in sight.'

At the word one of the three stepped forward a pace, and leaped twenty feet into the air; his great wings swung out as he leaped, they beat twice, and he went circling the hill in steady, noiseless flight.

He returned in a minute:

'There are no houses here, but a little way below I saw a fire and two people sitting beside it.'

'We will talk to them,' said the other. 'Show the way, Art.'

'Up then,' said Art.

'No,' said the Angel who had not yet spoken. 'I am tired of flying. We will walk to this place you speak of.'

'Very well,' replied Art, 'let us walk.'

And they went forward.

*

Around the little bucket of fire where Mac Cann and his daughter were sitting there was an intense darkness. At the distance of six feet they could still see, but delicately, indistinctly, and beyond that the night hung like a velvet curtain. They did not mind the night, they did not fear it, they did not look at it: it was around them, full of strangeness, full of mystery and terror, but they looked only at the glowing brazier, and in the red cheer of that they were content.

They had eaten the bread and the turnip, and were waiting for the potatoes to be cooked, and as they waited an odd phrase, an exclamation, a sigh would pass from one to the other; and then, suddenly, the dark curtain of night moved noiselessly, and the three angels stepped nobly in the firelight.

For an instant neither Mac Cann nor his daughter made a movement; they did not make a sound. Here was terror, and astonishment the sister of terror: they gaped: their whole being was in their eyes as they stared. From Mac Cann's throat came a noise; it had no grammatical significance, but it was weighted with all the sense that is in a dog's growl or a wolf's cry. Then the youngest of the strangers came forward:

'May we sit by your fire for a little time?' said he. 'The night is cold, and in this darkness one does not know where to go.'

At the sound of words Patsy seized hold of his sliding civilisation.

'To be sure,' he stammered. 'Why wouldn't your honour sit down? There isn't a seat, but you're welcome to the grass and the light of the fire.'

'Mary,' he continued, looking hastily around—

But Mary was not there. The same instant those tall forms strode from the darkness in front Mary had slipped, swift and noiseless as the shadow of a cat, into the darkness behind her.

'Mary,' said her father again, 'these are decent people, I'm thinking. Let you come from wherever you are, for I'm sure they wouldn't hurt yourself or myself.'

As swiftly as she had disappeared she reappeared.

'I was looking if the ass was all right,' said she sullenly.

She sat again by the brazier, and began to turn the potatoes with a stick. She did not appear to be taking any heed of the strangers, but it is likely that she was able to see them without looking, because, as is well known, women and birds are able to see without turning their heads, and that is indeed a necessary provision, for they are both surrounded by enemies.

CHAPTER III

THE remarkable thing about astonishment is that it can only last for an instant. No person can be surprised for more than that time. You will come to terms with a ghost within two minutes of its appearance, and it had scarcely taken that time for Mac Cann and his daughter to become one with the visitors.

If the surprisor and the surprisee are mutually astonished, then, indeed, there is a tangle out of which anything may emerge, for two explanations are necessary at the one moment, and two explanations can no more hold the same position in time than two bodies can occupy the same lodgment in space.

It needed alone that the angels should proclaim their quality for the situation to arrange itself naturally.

Man is a scientific creature; he labels his ignorance and shelves it: mystery affrights him, it bores him, but when he has given a name to any appearance then mystery flies away, and reality alone remains for his cogitation. Later, perhaps, reality will enrage and mystify him more profoundly than any unexpectedness can do.

The Mac Canns, so far as they professed a religion, were Catholics. Deeper than that they were Irish folk. From their cradles, if ever they had cradles other than a mother's breast and shoulder, they had supped on wonder. They believed as easily as an animal does, for most creatures are forced to credit everything long before they are able to prove anything. We have arranged to label these faculties of imagination and prophecy among the lesser creatures Instinct, and with the label we have thrown overboard more of mystery than we could afford to live with. Later these may confront us again in our proper souls, and the wonder and terror so long overdue will compel our tardy obeisance.

At the end of amazement, as of all else, we go to sleep, and, within an hour of their meeting, the angels and the Mac Canns were stretched in one common unconsciousness.

The angels were asleep—their attitudes proclaimed it. Patsy was asleep—his nose, with the unpleasant emphasis of a cracked trumpet, pealed wheezy confirmation of his slumber. His daughter was asleep, for there by the brazier she lay, motionless as the ground itself.

Perhaps she was not asleep. Perhaps she was lying with her face to the skies, staring through the darkness at the pale, scarce stars, dreaming dreams and seeing visions, while, all around, down the invisible road and across the vanished fields and the hills, night trailed her dusky robes and crushed abroad her poppy.

Whether she had slept or not she was the first to arise in the morning.

A pale twilight was creeping over the earth, and through it one could see chilly trees and shivering grass; the heavy clouds huddled together as though they were seeking warmth on those grisly heights; the birds had not yet left their nests; it was an hour of utter silence and uncomeliness; an hour for blind and despairing creatures to move forward spitefully, cursing themselves and the powers; an hour when imagination has no function, and hope would fly again to the darkness rather than remain in that livid wilderness, for this was not yet the thin child of the dawn, crowned with young buds and active as a wintry leaf, it was the abortion of the dawn, formless, heavy, and detestable.

Moving cautiously in that shade, Mary herself seemed no more than a shadow; she diminished thin and formless as a wraith, while she trod carefully to and fro from the cart to the hedge.

She sat down, unloosed her hair, and commenced to brush it.

In this colourless light her hair had no colour, but was of astonishing length and thickness; it flowed about her like a cloak, and as she sat it rolled and crept on the grass. She did not often tend her hair thus. Sometimes she plaited it for the sake of convenience, so that windy days would not whip it into her eyes or lash her cheeks; sometimes, through sheer laziness, she did not even plait it, she rolled it into a great ball and drew a wide, masculine cap over its brightness; and now, before the day had broken, sitting in a ghastly lightness, which was neither light nor darkness, she was attending to her hair.

And this hair perplexed her, for she did not know what to do with it; she did not know whether it was to be seen or not seen; whether to braid it in two great ropes, or roll it carelessly or carefully above her head, or let it hang loosely about her shoulders held only at the nape with a piece of ribbon or stuff. An hesitation such as this was new to her; she had never had occasion for such forethought; it was strange and inquieting; more disturbing, indeed, than the visit at black of night of those tall strangers whose eyes and voices were so quiet, and whose appointments flashed in the firelight while they spoke to her father of the things in which travellers are interested.

She looked at them where they lay, but they were scarcely more than visible—a tangle of flowing cloths and great limbs fading away in the rank grasses and the obscurity, and to her mind the real wonder was not that they had come, but that they were still there, and that they were sleeping deeply and peacefully as she had slept so often, with her head pillowed on her arm and her limbs folded calmly between the earth and the sky.

CHAPTER IV

HER hair was not braided; it was tied at the neck with a piece of whitish cloth torn from some part of her clothing, and upon her shoulders it billowed and rolled in magnificent living abundance.

Very gently she moved to where her father lay on his back with his mouth open and his black chin jutting at the sky. He was breathing through his mouth, so he was not snoring any longer. She lifted the three or four sacks which covered him, and rocked his shoulders cautiously until he awakened.

Her father awakened exactly as she did, exactly as every open-air animal does; his eyes flew wide, instantly and entirely wakeful, and he looked at her with full comprehension of their adventure. He raised softly on an elbow and glanced to where the strangers were; then nodded to his daughter and rose noiselessly to his feet. She beckoned him, and they stepped a few paces away so that they might talk in security.

Mary was about to speak but her father prevented her:

'Listen,' he whispered, 'the best thing we can do is to load the things into the cart, without making any noise, mind you! then we'll yoke the little ass as easy as anything, and then I'll get into the cart and I'll drive off as hard as ever I can pelt, and you can run beside the ass with a stick in your hand and you welting the devil out of him to make him go quick. I'm no good myself at the running, and that's why I'll get into the cart, but you can run like a hare, and that's why you'll wallop the beast.

'Mind now,' he continued fiercely, 'we don't know who them fellows are at all, and what would the priest say if he heard we were stravaiging the country with three big, buck angels, and they full of tricks maybe? so go you now and be lifting in the things and I'll give you good help myself.'

'I'll do nothing of the kind,' whispered Mary angrily, 'and it wasn't for that I woke you up.'

'Won't you, indeed?' said her father fiercely.

'What would they be thinking of us at all if they were to rouse and see us sneaking off in that way? I'm telling you now that I won't do it, and that you won't do it either, and if you make a move to the cart I'll give a shout that will waken the men.'

'The devil's in you, you strap!' replied her father, grinding his teeth at her. 'What call have we to be mixing ourselves up with holy angels that'll be killing us maybe in an hour or half an hour? and maybe they're not angels at all, but men that do be travelling the land in a circus and they full of fun and devilment?'

'It's angels they are,' replied his daughter urgently, 'and if they're not angels itself they are rich men, for there's big rings of gold on their fingers, and every ring has a diamond in it, and they've golden chains across their shoulders I'm telling you, and the stuff in their clothes is fit for the children of a king. It's rich and very rich they are.'

MacCann rasped his chin with his thumb.

'Do you think they are rich folk?'

'I do, indeed.'

'Then,' said her father in an abstracted tone, 'we won't say anything more about it.'

After a moment he spoke again:

'What were you thinking about yourself?'

'I was thinking,' she replied, 'that when they waken up in a little while there won't be anything at all for them to eat and they strangers.'

'Hum!' said her father.

'There's two cold potatoes in the basket,' she continued,

29

'and a small piece of bread, and there isn't anything more than that; so let you be looking around for something to eat the way we won't be put to shame before the men.'

'It's easy talking!' said he; 'where am I to look? Do you want me to pick red herrings out of the grass and sides of bacon off the little bushes?'

'We passed a house last night a mile down the road,' said Mary; 'go you there and get whatever you're able to get, and if you can't get anything buy it off the people in the house. I've three shillings in my pocket that I was saving for a particular thing, but I'll give them to you because I wouldn't like to be shamed before the strange men.'

Her father took the money:

'I wish I knew that you had it yesterday,' he growled, 'I wouldn't have gone to sleep with a throat on me like a mid-summer ditch and it full of dust and pismires.'

Mary pushed him down the road.

'Be back as quick as you are able, and buy every kind of thing that you can get for the three shillings.'

She watched him stamping heavily down the road, and then she returned again to their encampment.

CHAPTER V

THE visitors had not awakened.

Now the air was growing clearer; the first livid pallor of the dawn had changed to a wholesome twilight, and light was rolling like clear smoke over the land. The air looked cold, and it began to look sharp instead of muddy; now the trees and bushes stood apart; they seemed lonely and unguarded in that chill dawning; they seemed like living things which were cold and a little frightened in an immensity to which they were foreign and from which they had much to dread.

Of all unnatural things, if that word can be used in any context, there is none more unnatural than silence, there is none so terrifying; for silence means more than itself, it means also immobility; it is the symbol and signature of death, and from it no one knows what may come at an instant; for silence is not quietness, it is the enemy of quietness; against it your watch must climb the tower and stare in vain; against it your picket must be set, and he will thrust a lance to the sound of his own pulses; he will challenge the beating of his own heart, and hear his own harness threatening him at a distance.

To walk in a forest when there is no wind to stir the branches and set the leaves tapping upon the boughs, this is terrifying; a lonely sea stretching beyond sight and upon which there is no ripple holds the same despair, and a grassy plain from whence there is no movement visible has too its desolating horror.

But these things did not haunt the girl. She did not heed the silence for she did not listen to it; she did not heed the

31

immensity for she did not see it. In space and silence she had been cradled; they were her foster-parents, and if ever she looked or listened it was to see and hear something quite other than these. Now she did listen and look. She listened to the breathing of the sleepers, and soon, for she was a female, she looked to see what they were like.

She leaned softly over one. He was a noble old man with a sweeping, white beard and a great brow; the expression of his quiet features was that of a wise infant; her heart went out to him and she smiled at him in his sleep.

She trod to the next and bent again. He was younger, but not young; he looked about forty years of age; his features were regular and very determined; his face looked strong, comely as though it had been chiselled from a gracious stone; there was a short, coal-black beard on his chin.

She turned to the third sleeper, and halted blushing. She remembered his face, caught on the previous night in one lightning peep while she slid away from their approach. It was from him she had fled in the night, and for him that her hair was now draping her shoulders in unaccustomed beauty.

She did not dare go near him; she was afraid that if she bent over him he would flash open his eyes and look at her, and, as yet, she could not support such a look. She knew that if she were stretched in sleep and he approached to lean across her, she would awaken at the touch of his eyes, and she would be ashamed and frightened.

She did not look at him.

She went again to her place and set to building a fire in the brazier, and, while she sat, a voice began to sing in the dawn; not loud, but very gently, very sweetly. It was so early for a bird to sing, and she did not recognise that tune although the sound of it was thrilling through all her body. Softly, more softly, O Prophetic Voice! I do not know your speech; I do not know what happiness you are promising; is it of the

32

leaves you tell and of a nest that rocks high on a leafy spray; there your mate swings cooing to herself. She swings and coos; she is folded in peace, and the small, white clouds go sailing by and they do not fall.

So through unimagined ways went that song, lifting its theme in terms that she did not comprehend; but it was not a bird that sang to her, it was her own heart making its obscure music and lilting its secret, wild lyrics in the dawn.

CHAPTER VI

IT was the donkey awakened them.

For some time he had been rolling along the ground in ecstasy; now his agitated legs were pointing at the sky while he scratched his back against little stones and clumps of tough clay; now he was lying flat rubbing his jowl against these same clumps. He stood up suddenly, shook himself, swung up his tail and his chin, bared his teeth, fixed his eye on eternity, and roared 'hee-haw' in a voice of such sudden mightiness, that not alone did the sleepers bound from their slumbers, but the very sun itself leaped across the horizon and stared at him with its wild eye.

Mary ran and beat the ass on the nose with her fist, but whatever Mary did to the ass was understood by him as a caress, and he willingly suffered it—'hee-haw,' said he again triumphantly, and he planted his big head on her shoulder and stared sadly into space.

He was thinking, and thought always makes an ass look sad, but what he was thinking about not even Mary knew; his eye was hazy with cogitation, and he looked as wise and as kindly as the eldest of the three angels; indeed, although he had never been groomed, he looked handsome also, for he had the shape of a good donkey; his muzzle and his paws were white, the rest of his body was black, and his eyes were brown. That was the appearance of the donkey.

The angels arose and, much as the ass did, they shook themselves; there was no further toilet than that practicable; they ran their hands through their abundant hair, and the two who had beards combed these also with their fingers—then they looked around them.

34

Now the birds were sweeping and climbing on the shining air; they were calling and shrieking and singing; fifty of them, and all of the same kind, came dashing madly together, and they all sang the one song, so loud, so exultant, the heaven and earth seemed to ring and ring again of their glee.

They passed, and three antic wings came tumbling and flirting together; these had no song or their happiness went far beyond all orderly sound; they squealed as they chased each other; they squealed as they dropped twenty sheer feet towards the ground, and squealed again as they recovered on a swoop, and as they climbed an hundred feet in three swift zigzags, they still squealed without intermission, and then the three went flickering away to the west, each trying to bite the tail off the others.

There came a crow whose happiness was so intense that he was not able to move; he stood on the hedge for a long time, and all that time he was trying hard to compose himself to a gravity befitting the father of many families, but every few seconds he lost all control and bawled with fervour. He examined himself all over; he peeped under his feathers to see was his complexion good; he parted the plumage of his tail modishly; he polished his feet with his bill, and then polished his bill on his left thigh, and then he polished his left thigh with the back of his neck. 'I'm a hell of a crow,' said he, 'and everybody admits it.' He flew with admirable carelessness over the ass, and cleverly stole two claws and one beak full of hair; but in mid-air he laughed incautiously so that the hair fell out of his beak, and in grabbing at that portion he dropped the bits in his claws, and he got so excited in trying to rescue these before they reached the ground that his voice covered all the other sounds of creation.

The sun was shining; the trees waved their branches in delight; there was no longer murk or coldness in the air; it sparkled from every point like a vast jewel, and the brisk clouds arraying themselves in fleeces of white and blue raced happily aloft.

That was what the angels saw when they looked abroad; a few paces distant the cart was lying with its shafts up in the air, and a tumble of miscellaneous rubbish was hanging half in and half out of it; a little farther the ass, in a concentrated manner, was chopping grass as quickly as ever he could and, naturally enough, eating it; for after thinking deeply we eat, and it is true wisdom to do so.

The eldest of the angels observed the donkey. He stroked his beard.

'One eats that kind of vegetable,' said he.

The others observed also.

'And,' that angel continued, 'the time has come for us to eat.'

The second eldest angel rolled his coal-black chin in his hand, and his gesture and attitude were precisely those of Patsy Mac Cann.

'I am certainly hungry,' said he.

He picked a fistful of grass and thrust some of it into his mouth, but after a moment of difficulty he removed it again.

'It is soft enough to eat,' said he musingly, 'but I do not care greatly for its taste.'

The youngest angel made a suggestion.

'Let us talk to the girl,' said he.

And they all moved over to Mary.

'Daughter,' said the eldest of the three, 'we are hungry'; and he beamed on her so contentedly that all fear and diffidence fled from her on the instant.

She replied:

'My father has gone down the road looking for food; he will be coming back in a minute or two, and he'll be bringing every kind of thing that's nourishing.'

36

'While we are waiting for him,' said the angel, 'let us sit down and you can tell us all about food.'

'It is a thing we ought to learn at once,' said the second angel.

So they sat in a half-circle opposite the girl, and requested her to give them a lecture on food.

She thought it natural they should require information about earthly matters, but she found, as all unpractised speakers do, that she did not know at what point to begin on her subject. Still, something had to be said, for two of them were stroking their beards, and one was hugging his knees, and all three were gazing at her.

'Everything,' said she, 'that a body can eat is good to eat, but some things do taste nicer than others; potatoes and cabbage are very good to eat, and so is bacon; my father likes bacon when it's very salt, but I don't like it that way myself; bread is a good thing to eat, and so is cheese.'

'What do you call this vegetable that the animal is eating?' said the angel, pointing to the ass.

'That isn't a vegetable at all, sir, that's only grass; every kind of animal eats it, but Christians don't.'

'Is it not good to eat?'

'Sure, I don't know. Dogs eat it when they are sick, so it ought to be wholesome, but I never heard tell of any person that ate grass except they were dying of the hunger and couldn't help themselves, poor creatures! And there was a Jew once who was a king, and they do say that he used to go out with the cattle and eat the grass like themselves, and nobody says that he didn't get fat.

'But here's my father coming across the fields (which is a queer way for him to come because he went away by the road), and I'm thinking that he has a basket under his arm and there will be food in it.'

37

CHAPTER VII

IT was true enough. Mac Cann was coming to them from a
point at right angles to where he was expected.

Now and again he turned to look over his shoulder, and
as he was taking advantage of dips in the ground, bushes,
and such-like to shield his advance, his daughter divined that
something had occurred in addition to the purchase of food.
She had often before observed her father moving with these
precautionary tactics, and had many times herself shared
and even directed a retreat which was full of interest.

When her father drew nigh he nodded meaningly at her,
set down a basket and a bundle, and stood for a moment
looking at these while he thumbed his chin.

'Faith!' said he, 'the world is full of trouble, and that's a
fact.'

He turned to the strangers.

'And I'm telling you this, that if the world wasn't full of
trouble there'd be no life at all for the poor. It's the only
chance we get is when people are full of woe, God help them!
and isn't that a queer thing?

'Mary'—he turned, and his voice was full of careless pride
—'try if there isn't some small thing or other in the basket;
and let your honours sit down on the grass while the young
girl is getting your breakfast.'

So the angels and Patsy sat down peacefully on the grass,
and Mary opened the basket.

There were two loaves of bread in it, a fine square of
butter, a piece of cheese as big as a man's hand and four
times as thick; there was a leg of mutton in the basket, and

only a little bit had been taken off it; a big paper bag full of tea, a package of soft sugar, a bottle full of milk, a bottle half full of whisky, two tobacco pipes having silver bands on their middles, and a big bar of plug tobacco. Those were the things in the basket.

Mary's eyes and her mouth opened when she saw them, and she blessed herself, but she made no sound; and when she turned her face towards the company there was no expression on it except that of hospitality.

She cut slices from each of these things and piled them on a large piece of paper in the centre of the men; then she sat herself down and they all prepared to eat.

The second angel turned courteously to Mac Cann.

'Will you kindly begin to eat,' said he, 'and by watching you we will know what to do?'

'There can be nothing more uncomely,' said the first angel, 'than to see people acting in disaccord with custom; we will try to do exactly as you do, and although you may be troubled by our awkwardness you will not be shocked by a lapse from sacred tradition.'

'Well!' said Patsy thoughtfully.

He stretched a hand towards the food.

'I'll stand in nobody's light, and teaching people is God's own work; this is the way I do it, your worships, and any one that likes can follow me up.'

He seized two pieces of bread, placed a slice of cheese between them, and bit deeply into that trinity.

The strangers followed his actions with fidelity, and in a moment their mouths were as full as his was and as content.

Patsy paused between bites:

'When I've this one finished,' said he, 'I'll take two more bits of bread and I'll put a lump of meat between them, and I'll eat that.'

39

'Ah!' said that one of the angels whose mouth chanced to be free.

Patsy's eye roved over the rest of the food.

'And after that,' he continued, 'we will take a bit of whatever is handy.'

In a short time there was nothing left on the newspaper but soft sugar, butter, tea, and tobacco. Patsy was abashed.

'I did think that there was more than that,' said he.

'I've had enough myself,' he continued, 'but maybe your honours could eat more.'

Two of the angels assured him that they were quite satisfied, but the youngest angel said nothing.

'I'm doubting that you had enough,' said Patsy dubiously to him.

'I could eat more if I had it,' returned that one, with a smile.

Mary went to the cart and returned bearing two cold potatoes and a piece of bread, and she placed these before the young angel. He thanked her and ate these, and then he ate the package of soft sugar, and then he ate a little piece of the butter, but he didn't care for it. He pointed to the plug of tobacco:

'Does this be eaten?' he enquired.

'It does not,' said Patsy. 'If you ate a bit of that you'd get a pain inside of your belly that would last you for a month. There's some people do smoke it, and there's others do chew it; but I smoke it and chew it myself, and that's the best way. There's two pipes there on the paper, and I've a pipe in my own pocket, so whichever of you would like a smoke can do exactly as I do.'

With a big jack-knife he shredded pieces from the plug, and rolled these between his palms, then he carefully stuffed his pipe, pulled at it to see was it drawing well, lit the tobacco, and heaved a sigh of contentment. He smiled around the circle.

40

'That's real good,' said he.

The strangers examined the pipes and tobacco with curiosity, but they did not venture to smoke, and they watched Patsy's beatific face with kindly attention.

CHAPTER VIII

NOW at this moment Mary was devoured with curiosity. She wanted to know how her father had become possessed of the basketful of provisions. She knew that three shillings would not have purchased a tithe of these goods, and, as she had now no fear of the strangers, she questioned her parent.

'Father,' said she, 'where did you get all the good food?'

The angels had eaten of his bounty, so Mac Cann considered that he had nothing to fear from their side. He regarded them while he pulled thoughtfully at his pipe.

'Do you know,' said he, 'that the hardest thing in the world is to get the food, and a body is never done looking for it. We are after eating all that we got this morning, so now we'll have to search for what we'll eat to-night, and in the morning we'll have to look again for more of it, and the day after that, and every day until we are dead we'll have to go on searching for the food.'

'I would have thought,' said the eldest angel, 'that of all problems food would be the simplest in an organised society.'

This halted Mac Cann for a moment.

'Maybe you're right, sir,' said he kindly, and he dismissed the interruption.

'I heard a man once—he was a stranger to these parts, and he had a great deal of the talk—he said that the folk at the top do grab all the food in the world, and that then they make every person work for them, and that when you've done a certain amount of work they give you just enough money to buy just enough food to let you keep on working for them. That's what the man said: a big, angry man he was

42

with whiskers on him like the whirlwind, and he swore he wouldn't work for any one. I'm thinking myself that he didn't work either. We were great friends, that man and me, for I don't do any work if I can help it; it's that I haven't got the knack for work, and, God help me! I've a big appetite. Besides that, the work I'd be able to do in a day mightn't give me enough to eat, and wouldn't I be cheated then?'

'Father,' said Mary, 'where did you get all the good food this morning?'

'I'll tell you that. I went down to the bend of the road where the house is, and I had the three shillings in my hand. When I came to the house the door was standing wide open. I hit it a thump of my fist, but nobody answered me. 'God be with all here,' said I, and in I marched. There was a woman lying on the floor in one room, and her head had been cracked with a stick; and in the next room there was a man lying on the floor, and his head had been cracked with a stick. It was in that room I saw the food packed nice and tight in the basket that you see before you. I looked around another little bit, and then I came away, for, as they say, a wise man never found a dead man, and I'm wise enough no matter what I look like.'

'Were the people all dead?' said Mary, horrified.

'They were not—they only got a couple of clouts. I'm thinking they are all right by this, and they looking for the basket, but, please God, they won't find it. But what I'd like to know is this, who was it hit the people with a stick, and then walked away without the food and the drink and the tobacco, for that's a queer thing?'

He turned to his daughter:

'Mary, a cree, let you burn up that basket in the brazier, for I don't like the look of it at all, and it empty.'

So Mary burned the basket with great care while her father piled their goods on the cart and yoked up the ass.

Meanwhile the angels were talking together, and after a short time they approached Mac Cann.

'If it is not inconvenient,' said their spokesman, 'we would like to remain with you for a time. We think that in your company we may learn more than we might otherwise do, for you seem to be a man of ability, and at present we are rather lost in this strange world.'

'Sure,' said Patsy heartily, 'I haven't the least objection in the world, only, if you don't want to be getting into trouble, and if you'll take my advice, I'd say that ye ought to take off them kinds of clothes you're wearing and get into duds something like my own; and let you put your wings aside and your fine high crowns the way folk won't be staring at you every foot of the road, for I'm telling you that it's a bad thing to have people looking after you when you go through a little village or a town, because you can never know who'll remember you afterwards, and you maybe not wanting to be remembered at all.'

'If our attire,' said the angel, 'is such as would make us remarkable—'

'It is,' said Patsy. 'People would think you belonged to a circus, and the crowds of the world would be after you in every place.'

'Then,' replied the angel, 'we will do as you say.'

'I have clothes enough in this bundle,' said Patsy, with a vague air. 'I found them up there in the house, and I was thinking of yourselves when I took them. Let you put them on, and we will tie up your own things in a sack and bury them here so that when you want them again you'll be able to get them, and then we can travel wherever we please and no person will say a word to us.'

So the strangers retired a little way with the bundle, and there they shed their finery.

When they appeared again they were clad in stout, ordinary clothing. They did not look a bit different from

Patsy Mac Cann except that they were all taller men than he, but between his dilapidation and theirs there was very little to choose.

Mac Cann dug a hole beside a tree and carefully buried their property, then with a thoughtful air he bade Mary move ahead with the ass, while he and the angels stepped forward at the tailboard.

They walked then through the morning sunlight, and for a time they had little to say to each other.

CHAPTER IX

In truth Patsy Mac Cann was a very able person.

For forty-two years he had existed on the edges of a society which did not recognise him in any way, and, as he might himself have put it, he had not done so very badly at all.

He lived as a bird lives, or a fish, or a wolf. Laws were for other people, but they were not for him; he crawled under or vaulted across these ethical barriers, and they troubled him no more than as he had to bend or climb a little to avoid them—he discerned laws as something to be avoided, and it was thus he saw most things.

Religion and morality, although he paid these an extra-ordinary reverence, were not for him either; he beheld them from afar, and, however they might seem beautiful or foolish, he left them behind as readily as he did his debts, if so weighty a description may be given to his volatile engagements. He did not discharge these engagements; he elongated himself from them; between himself and a query he interposed distance, and at once that became foreign to him, for half a mile about himself was his frontier, and beyond that, wherever he was, the enemy lay.

He stood outside of every social relation, and within an organised humanity he might almost have been reckoned as a different species. He was very mobile, but all his freedom lay in one direction, and outside of that pasturage he could never go. For the average man there are two dimensions of space wherein he moves with a certain limited freedom; it is for him a horizontal and a perpendicular world; he goes up the social scale and down it, and in both these atmospheres there is a level wherein he can exercise himself to and fro, his journeyings being strictly limited by his business and his family. Between the place where he works and the place where he lives lies all the freedom he can hope for; within that range he must seek such adventures as he craves, and the sole expansion to which he can attain is upwards towards another social life if he be ambitious, or downward to the underworlds if he is bored. For Mac Cann there were no upward and no downward movements, he had plumbed to the very rocks of life, but his horizontal movements were bounded only by the oceans around his country, and in this gigantic underworld he moved with almost absolute freedom, and a knowledge which might properly be termed scientific.

In despite of his apparent outlawry he was singularly secure; ambition waved no littlest lamp at him; the one ill which could overtake him was death, which catches on every man; no enmity could pursue him to any wall, for he was sunken a whole sphere beneath malice as beneath benevolence. Physical ill-treatment might come upon him, but in that case it was his manhood and his muscle against another manhood and another muscle—the simplest best would win, but there was no glory for the conqueror nor any loot to be carried from the battle.

Casual warfares, such as these, had been frequent enough in his career, for he had fought stubbornly with every kind of man, and had afterwards medicined his wounds with the only unguents cheap enough for his usage—the healing balsams of time and patience. He had but one occupation, and it was an engrossing one—he hunted for food, and for it he hunted with the skill and pertinacity of a wolf or a vulture.

With what skill he did hunt! He would pick crumbs from the lank chaps of famine; he gathered nourishment from the empty air; he lifted it from wells and watercourses; he picked it off clothes-lines and hedges; he stole so cleverly from the

47

bees that they never felt his hand in their pocket; he would lift the eggs from beneath a bird, and she would think that his finger was a chicken; he would clutch a hen from the roost, and the housewife would think he was the yard dog, and the yard dog would think he was its brother.

He had a culture too, and if it was not wide it was profound; he knew wind and weather as few astronomers know it; he knew the habit of the trees and the earth; how the seasons moved, not as seasons, but as days and hours; he had gathered all the sweets of summer, and the last rigour of winter was no secret to him; he had fought with the winter every year of his life as one fights with a mad beast, he had held off that grizzliest of muzzles and escaped scatheless.

He knew men and women, and he knew them from an angle at which they seldom caught themselves or each other; he knew them as prey to be bitten and escaped from quickly. At them, charged with a thousand preoccupations, he looked with an eye in which there was a single surmise, and he divined them in a flash. In this quick vision he saw man, one expression, one attitude for all; never did he see a man or woman in their fullness, his microscopic vision caught only what it looked for, but he saw that with the instant clarity of the microscope. There were no complexities for him in humanity; there were those who gave and those who did not give; there were those who might be cajoled, and those who might be frightened. If there was goodness in a man he glimpsed it from afar as a hawk sees a mouse in the clover, and he swooped on that virtue and was away with booty. If there was evil in a man he passed it serenely as a sheep passes by a butcher, for evil did not affect him. Evil could never put a hand on him, and he was not evil himself.

If the denominations of virtue or vice must be affixed to his innocent existence, then these terms would have to be redefined for they had no meaning in his case; he stood outside these as he did outside of the social structure. But, indeed, he was not outside of the social structure at all; he was so far inside of it that he could never get out; he was at the very heart of it; he was held in it like a deer in an ornamental park, or a cork that bobs peacefully in a bucket, and in the immense, neglected pastures of civilisation he found his own quietude and his own wisdom.

All of the things he knew and all of the things that he had done were most competently understood by his daughter.

CHAPTER X

IT is to be remarked that the angels were strangely like Patsy
Mac Cann. Their ideas of right and wrong almost entirely
coincided with his. They had no property and so they had no
prejudices, for the person who has nothing may look upon
the world as his inheritance, while the person who has something has seldom anything but that.

Civilisation, having built itself at hazard upon the Rights
of Property, has sought on many occasions to unbuild itself
again in sheer desperation of any advance, but from the
great Ethic of Possession there never has been any escape,
and there never will be until the solidarity of man has been
really created, and until each man ceases to see the wolf in
his neighbour.

Is there actually a wolf in our neighbour? We see that
which we are, and our eyes project on every side an image of
ourselves; if we look with fear, that which we behold is
frightful; if we look with love, then the colours of heaven are
repeated to us from the ditch and the dungeon. We invent
eternally upon one another; we scatter our sins broadcast
and call them our neighbours'; let us scatter our virtues
abroad and build us a city to live in.

For Mac Cann and his daughter there was no longer any
strangeness in their companions. As day and night suceeded,
as conversation and action supplemented each other on
their journeys, so each of them began to unfold from the
fleshy disguise, and in a short time they could each have
spoken of the others to an enquiring stranger, giving, within
bounds, reasonably exact information as to habit and
mentality.

What conversations they had engaged in! Sitting now by a hedge close to a tiny chaotic village, compact of ugliness and stupidity, now at twilight as they camped in a disused quarry, leaning their shoulders against great splintered rocks, and hearing no sound but the magnified, slow trickle of water and the breeze that sung or screamed against a razor-edge of rock; or lying on the sheltered side of a pit of potatoes, they stared at the moon as she sailed on her lonely voyages, or watched the stars that glanced and shone from the drifting clouds; and as they lifted their eyes to these sacred voyagers in whose charge is the destiny of man they lifted their minds also and adored mutely that mind of which these are the thoughts made visible.

Sometimes they discussed the problems of man in a thousand superficial relationships. The angels were wise, but in the vocabulary which they had to use wisdom had no terms. Their wisdom referred only to ultimates, and was the unhandiest of tools when dug into some immediate, curious problem. Before wisdom can be audible a new language must be invented, and they also had to unshape their definitions and re-translate these secular findings into terms wherein they could see the subject broadly, and they found that what they gained in breadth they lost in outline, and that the last generalisation, however logically it was framed, was seldom more than an intensely interesting lie when it was dissected again. No truth in regard to space and time can retain virtue for longer than the beating of an artery; it too has its succession, its sidereal tide, and while you look upon it, round and hardy as a pebble, behold, it is split and fissured and transformed.

Sometimes when it rained, and it rained often, they would seek refuge in a haystack, if one was handy; or they would creep into a barn and hide behind hills of cabbages or piles of farming tools; or they slid into the sheds among the cattle, where they warmed and fed themselves against those peaceful flanks; or, if they were nigh a town and had been lucky that day, they would pay a few coppers to sleep on the well-trodden, earthen floor of a house.

As for the ass, he slept wherever he could. When there was rain he would stand with his tail against the wind sunken in a reverie so profound that he no longer seemed to feel the rain or the wind. From these abysses of thought he would emerge to the realisation that there was a sheltered side to a wall or a clump of heather, and he also would take his timely rest under the stars of God.

What did they say to him? Down the glittering slopes they peer and nod; before his eyes the mighty pageant is unrolled in quiet splendour; for him too the signs are set. Does the Waterman care nothing for his thirst? Does the Ram not bless his increase? Against his enemies also the Archer will bend his azure bow and loose his arrows of burning gold.

On their journeyings they met with many people; not the folk who lived in the houses dotted here and there at great distances from each other on the curving roads, for with these people they had nothing to do, they had scarcely anything to say, and the housefolk looked on the strollers with a suspicion which was almost a fear. The language of these was seldom gracious, and often, on their approach, the man of the house was sent for and the dog was unchained.

But for the vagabonds these people did not count; Mac Cann and his daughter scarcely looked on them as human beings, and if he had generalised about them at all, he would have said that there was no difference between these folk and the trees that shaded their dwellings in leafy spray, that they were rooted in their houses, and that they had no idea of life other than the trees might have which snuff for ever the same atmosphere and look on the same horizon until they droop again to the clay they lifted from.

It was with quite other people they communed.

The wandering ballad-singer with his wallet of songs

slung at his ragged haunch; the travelling musician whose blotchy fiddle could sneeze out the ten strange tunes he had learned from his father and from his father's generations before him; the little band travelling the world carrying saplings and rushes from the stream which they wove cunningly into tables and chairs warranted not to last too long; the folk who sold rootless ferns to people from whose window-ledges they had previously stolen the pots to plant them in; the men who went roaring along the roads driving the cattle before them from fair to market and back again; the hairy tinkers with their clattering metals, who marched in the angriest of battalions and who spoke a language composed entirely of curses.

These, and an hundred varieties of these, they met and camped with and were friendly with, and to the angels these people were humanity, and the others were, they did not know what.

CHAPTER XI

IT might be asked why Patsy Mac Cann permitted the strangers to remain with him.

Now that they were dressed like himself he had quite forgotten, or he never thought of their celestial character, and they were undoubtedly a burden upon his ingenuity. They ate as vigorously as he did, and the food which they ate he had to supply.

There were two reasons for this kindliness—He had always wished to be the leader of a troop. In his soul the Ancient Patriarch was alive and ambitious of leadership. Had his wife given him more children he would have formed them and their wives and children into a band, and the affairs of this little world would have been directed by him with pride and pleasure. He would have observed their goings-out and their comings-in; he would have apportioned praise and reproach to his little clann; he would have instructed them upon a multitude of things, and passed on to them the culture which he had gathered so hardily, and, when they arrived at the age of ingenuity, it would have still been his ambition to dash their arguments with his superior knowledge, or put the happy finish to any plan which they submitted for his approval; he would have taken the road, like a prince of old, with his tail, and he would have undertaken such raids and forays that his name and fame would ring through the underworld like the note of a trumpet.

He could not do this because he only had one child (the others had died wintry deaths) and she was a girl. But now Heaven itself had blessed him with a following and he led it with skill and enjoyment. Furthermore, his daughter, of whom he stood in considerable awe, had refused flatly to desert the strangers whom Providence had directed to them.

She had constituted herself in some strange way the mother of the four men. She cooked for them, she washed and mended for them, and, when the necessity arose, she scolded them with the heartiest good-will.

Her childhood had known nothing of dolls, and so her youth made dolls of these men whom she dressed and fed. Sometimes her existence with them was peaceful and happy; at other times she almost went mad with jealous rage. Little by little she began to demand a domestic obedience which they very willingly gave her; so they were her men and no one else's, and the exercise of this power gave her a delight such as she had never known.

She was wise also for it was only in domestic affairs that she claimed their fealty; with their masculine movements she did not interfere, nor did she interfere with the task and apportioning of the day, although her counsel was willingly listened to in these matters; but when night came, when the camp was selected, the little cart unloaded, and the brazier lit, then she stepped briskly to her kingdom and ruled like a chieftainess.

With her father she often had trouble: he would capitulate at the end, but not until he had set forth at length his distaste for her suggestions and his assurance that she was a strap. She seldom treated him as a father, for she seldom remembered that relationship; she loved him as one loves a younger brother, and she was angry with him as one can only be angry with a younger brother. Usually she treated him as an infant; she adored him, and, if he had permitted it, she would have beaten him soundly on many an occasion.

For she was a strong girl. She was big in build and bone, and she was beautiful and fearless. Framed in a rusty shawl her face leaped out instant and catching as a torch in darkness; under her clumsy garments one divined a body to be adored as a revelation; she walked carelessly as the wind walks, proudly as a young queen trained in grandeur. She could leap from where she stood, as a wild-cat that springs terribly from quietude; she could run as a deer runs, and pause at full flight like a carven statue. Each movement of hers was complete and lovely in itself; when she lifted a hand to her hair the free attitude was a marvel of composure; it might never have begun, and might never cease, it was solitary and perfect; when she bent to the brazier she folded to such an economy of content that one might have thought her half her size and yet perfect; she had that beauty which raises the mind of man to an ecstasy which is murderous if it be not artistic; and she was so conscious of her loveliness that she could afford to forget it, and so careless that she had never yet used it as a weapon or a plea.

She could not but be aware of her beauty, for her mirrors had tongues; they were the eyes of those she met and paused with. No man had yet said anything to her, saving in rough jest as to a child, but no woman could speak of anything else in her presence, and these exclamations drummed through all their talk.

She had been worshipped by many women, for to physical loveliness in their own sex women are the veriest slaves. They will love a man for his beauty, but a woman they will adore as a singularity, as something almost too good to be true, as something which may vanish even while they gaze at it. Prettiness they understand and like or antagonise, but they have credited beauty as a masculine trait, and as a race long sunken in slavery, and who look almost despairingly for a saviour, so the female consciousness prostrates itself before female beauty as before a Messiah who will lead them to the unconscious horrible ambitions which are the goal of femininity. But, and it is humanity's guard against a solitary development, while women worship a beautiful woman the beauty does not care for them; she accepts their homage and flies them as one flies from the deadliest boredom; she is the widest swing of their pendulum, and must hurry again from the circumference to the centre with the violent speed of an outcast who sees from afar the smoke of his father's house and the sacred roof-tree.

There is a steadying influence; an irreconcilable desire and ambition; the desire of every woman to be the wife of a fool, her ambition to be the mother of a genius; but they postulate genius, it is their outlet and their justification for that leap at a tangent which they have already taken.

Out there they have discovered the Neuter. Is the Genius always to be born from an unfertilised womb, or rather a self-fertilised one? Singular Messiahs! scorners of paternity! claiming no less than the Cosmos for a father; taking from the solitary mother capacity for infinite suffering and infinite love, whence did ye gather the rough masculine intellect, the single eye, all that hardiness of courage and sensibility of self that made of your souls a battlefield, and of your memory a terror to drown love under torrents of horrid red! Deluded so far and mocked! No genius has yet sprung from ye but the Genius of War and Destruction, those frowning captains that have ravaged our vineyards and blackened our generations with the torches of their egotism.

To woman beauty is energy, and they would gladly take from their own sex that which they have so long accepted from man. They are economical; the ants and the bees are not more amazingly parsimonious than they, and, like the ants and the bees, their subsequent extravagance is a thing to marvel at. Food and children they will hoard, and when these are safeguarded their attitude to the life about them is ruinous. They will adorn themselves at the expense of all creation, and in a few years they crush from teeming life a species which nature has toiled through laborious ages to perfect. They adorn themselves, and too often adornment is the chief manifestation of boredom. They are world-weary, sex-weary, and they do not know what they want; but they want power, so that they may rule evolution once more as long ago they ruled it; their blood remembers an ancient greatness; they crave to be the queens again, to hold the sceptre of life in their cruel hands, to break up the mould which has grown too rigid for freedom, to form anew the chaos which is a womb, and which they conceive is their womb, and to create therein beauty and freedom and power. But the king whom they have placed on the throne has grown wise in watching them; he is their bone terribly separated, terribly endowed; he uses their cruelty, their fierceness, as his armies against them—and so the battle is set, and wild deeds may flare from the stars of rebellion and prophecy.

Mary, who could make women do anything for her, was entirely interested in making men bow to her will, and because, almost against her expectation, they did bow, she loved them, and could not sacrifice herself too much for their comfort or even their caprice. It was the mother-spirit in her which, observing the obedience of her children, is forced in very gratitude to become their slave; for, beyond all things, a woman desires power, and, beyond all things, she is unable to use it when she gets it. If this power be given to her grudgingly she will exercise it mercilessly; if it is given kindly, then she is bound by her nature to renounce authority, and to live happy ever after, but it must be given to her.

CHAPTER XII

IT may be surprising to learn that the names of the angels were Irish names, but more than eight hundred years ago a famous Saint informed the world that the language spoken in heaven was Gaelic, and, presumably, he had information on the point. He was not an Irishman, and he had no reason to exalt Fodhla above the other nations of the earth, and, therefore, his statement may be accepted on its merits, the more particularly as no other saint has denied it, and every Irish person is prepared to credit it.

It was also believed in ancient times, and the belief was world-wide, that the entrance to heaven, hell, and purgatory yawned in the Isle of the Saints, and this belief also, although it has never been proved, has never been disproved, and it does assist the theory that Irish is the celestial language. Furthermore, Gaelic is the most beautiful and expressive fashion of speech in the whole world, and, thus, an artistic and utilitarian reinforcement can be hurried to the support of that theory should it ever be in danger from philologists with foreign axes to grind.

The names of the angels were Finaun and Caeltia and Art.

Finaun was the eldest angel; Caeltia was that one who had a small coal-black beard on his chin, and Art was the youngest of the three, and he was as beautiful as the dawn, than which there is nothing more beautiful.

Finaun was an Archangel when he was in his own place; Caeltia was a Seraph, and Art was a Cherub. An Archangel is a Councillor and a Guardian; a Seraph is one who accumulates knowledge; a Cherub is one who accumulates love. In heaven these were their denominations.

Finaun was wise, childish, and kind, and between him and the little ass which drew their cart there was a singular and very pleasant resemblance.

Caeltia was dark and determined, and if he had cropped his beard with a scissors, the way Patsy Mac Cann did, he would have resembled Patsy Mac Cann as closely as one man can resemble another.

Art was dark also, and young and swift and beautiful. Looking carelessly at him one would have said that, barring the colour, he was the brother of Mary Mac Cann, and that the two of them were born at a birth, and a good birth.

Mary extended to Finaun part of the affection which she already had for the ass, and while they were marching the roads these three always went together; the archangel would be on one side of the donkey and Mary would be on the other side, and (one may say so) the three of them never ceased talking for an instant.

The ass, it will be admitted, did not speak, but he listened with such evident intention that no one could say he was out of the conversation; his right-hand ear hearkened agilely to Mary; his left-hand ear sprang to attention when Finaun spoke, and when, by a chance, they happened to be silent at the one moment, then both his ears drooped forward towards his nose, and so he was silent also. A hand from either side continually touched his muzzle caressingly, and at moments entirely unexpected he would bray affectionately at them in a voice that would have tormented the ears of any but a true friend.

Patsy Mac Cann and the seraph Caeltia used to march exactly at the tail of the cart, and they, also, talked a lot.

At first Patsy talked the most, for he had much information to impart, and the seraph listened with intent humility; but, after a while, Caeltia, having captured knowledge, would dispute and argue with great vivacity. They spoke of many things, but a person who listened closely and recorded these things would have found that they talked oftener about strong drinks than about anything else. Mac Cann used to speak longingly about strange waters which he had heard were brewed in foreign lands, potent brewings which had been described to him by emphatic sailormen with tarry thumbs; but at this stage Caeltia only spoke about porter and whisky, and was well contented to talk of these.

The cherub Art was used to promenade alone behind them all, but sometimes he would go in front and listen to the conversation with the ass; sometimes he would join the two behind and force them to consider matters in which they were not interested; and sometimes again he would range the fields on either side, or he would climb a tree, or he would go alone by himself shouting a loud song that he had learned at the fair which they had last journeyed to, or he would prance silently along the road as though his body was full of jumps and he did not know what to do with them, or he would trudge forlornly in a boredom so profound that one expected him to drop dead of it in his tracks.

So life fell into a sort of routine.

When they were camped for the night Caeltia and Art would always sit on one side of the brazier with Patsy Mac Cann sitting between them; on the other side of the brazier the archangel and Mary would sit; Finaun always sat very close to her when they had finished eating and were all talking together; he used to take her long plait of hair into his lap, and for a long time he would unplait and plait again the end of that lovely rope.

Mary liked him to do this, and nobody else minded it.

BOOK II
EILEEN NI COOLEY

CHAPTER XIII

EARLY in the morning the sun had been shining gloriously, and there was a thump of a wind blowing across the road that kept everything gay; the trees were in full leaf and every bough went jigging to its neighbour, but on the sky the clouds raced so fast that they were continually catching each other up and getting so mixed that they could not disentangle themselves again, and from their excessive gaiety black misery spread and the sun took a gloomy cast.

Mac Cann screwed an eye upwards like a bird and rubbed at his chin.

'There will be rain soon,' said he, 'and the country wants it.'

'It will be heavy rain,' said his daughter.

'It will so,' he replied; 'let us be getting along now the way we'll be somewhere before the rain comes, for I never did like getting wetted by rain, and nobody ever did except the people of the County Cork, and they are so used to it that they never know whether it's raining or whether it isn't.'

So they encouraged the ass to go quicker and he did that.

As they hastened along the road they saw in front of them two people marching close together, and in a little time they drew close to these people.

'I know the look of that man's back,' said Patsy, 'but I can't tell you where I saw it. I've a good memory for faces though, and I'll tell you all about him in a minute.'

'Do you know the woman that is with him?' said Caeltia.

'You can't tell a woman by her back,' replied Patsy, 'and nobody could, for they all have the same back when they have a shawl on.'

Mary turned her head to them:

'Every woman's back is different,' said she, 'whether there's a shawl on it or not, and I know from the way that woman is wearing her shawl that she is Eileen Ni Cooley and no one else.'

'If that is so,' said her father hastily, 'let us be going slower the way we won't catch up on her. Mary, a grah, whisper a word in the ass's ear so that he won't be going so quick, for he is full of fun this day.'

'I'll do that,' said Mary, and she said 'whoa' into the ear of the little ass, and he stopped inside the quarter of a pace.

'Do you not like that woman?' Caeltia enquired.

'She's a bad woman,' replied Patsy.

'What sort of a bad woman is she?'

'She's the sort that commits adultery with every kind of man,' said he harshly.

Caeltia turned over that accusation for a moment.

'Did she ever commit adultery with yourself?' said he.

'She did not,' said Patsy, 'and that's why I don't like her.'

Caeltia considered that statement also, and found it reasonable:

'I think,' said he, 'that the reason you don't like that woman is because you like her too much.'

'It's so,' said Patsy, 'but there is no reason for her taking on with every kind of man and not taking on with me at all.'

He was silent for a moment.

'I tell you,' said he furiously, 'that I made love to that woman from the dawn to the dark, and then she walked off with a man that came down a little road.'

'That was her right,' said Caeltia mildly.

'Maybe it was, but for the weight of a straw I would have killed the pair of them that night in the dark place.'

'Why didn't you?'

'She had me weakened. My knees gave under me when she walked away, and there wasn't even a curse in my mouth.'

Again he was silent, and again he broke into angry speech:

'I don't want to see her at all for she torments me, so let the pair of them walk their road until they come to a ditch that is full of thorns and is fit for them to die in.'

'I think,' said Caeltia, 'that the reason you don't want to see her is because you want to see her too much.'

'It's so,' growled Mac Cann, 'and it's so too that you are a prying kind of a man and that your mouth is never at rest, so we'll go on now to the woman yonder, and let you talk to her with your tongue and your nimble questions.'

Thereupon he rushed forward and kicked the ass so suddenly in the belly that it leaped straight off the ground and began to run before its legs touched earth again.

When they had taken a few dozen steps Mac Cann began to roar furiously:

'What way are you, Eileen Ni Cooley? What sort of a man is it that's walking beside yourself?'

And he continued roaring questions such as that until they drew on the people.

The folk stopped at his shouts.

The woman was big and thin and she had red hair. Her face was freckled all over so that one could only see her delicate complexion in little spots, and at the first glance the resemblance between herself and Finaun was extraordinary. In the sweep of the brow, the set of the cheek-bones, a regard of the eyes, that resemblance was seen, and then the look vanished in a poise of the head and came again in another one.

At the moment her blue eyes seemed the angriest that ever were in a woman's head. She stood leaning on a thick ash-plant and watched the advancing company, but she did not utter a word to them.

The man by her side was tall also and as thin as a pole; he was ramshackle and slovenly; there was not much pith in his body, for he was weak at the knees and his big feet splayed outwards at a curious angle; but his face was extraordinarily intelligent, and when he was younger must have been beautiful. Drink and ill-health had dragged and carved his flesh, and nothing of comeliness remained to him but his eyes, which were timid and tender as those of a fawn, and his hands which had never done anything but fumble with women. He also leaned quietly on a cudgel and watched Patsy Mac Cann.

And it was to him that Patsy came. He did not look once at the woman, though all the time he never ceased shouting salutations and questions at her by her name.

He walked directly to the man, eyeing him intently.

'And how is yourself?' he roared with horrible heartiness. 'It's a while since I saw you, and it was the pitch night that time.'

'I'm all right,' said the man.

'So you are,' said Patsy, 'and why wouldn't you be? Weren't you born in the wide lap of good luck, and didn't you stay there? Ah, it's the way that the men that come down little, narrow paths do have fortune, and the ones that tramp the wide roads do have nothing but their broken feet. Good luck to you, my soul, and long may you wave —Eh!'

'I didn't say a word,' said the man.

'And there's a stick in your hand that would crack the skull of a mountain, let alone a man.'

'It's a good stick,' said the man.

'Would you be calling it the brother or the husband of the one that the woman has in her happy hands?'

'I would be calling it a stick only,' replied the man.

'That's the name for it surely,' said Patsy, 'for a stick hasn't got a soul any more than a woman has, and isn't that a great mercy and a great comfort, for heaven would be full of women and wood, and there would be no room for the men and the drink.'

The red-haired woman strode to Patsy and, putting her hand against his breast, she gave him a great push:

'If you're talking,' said she, 'or if you're fighting, turn to myself, for the man doesn't know you.'

—Patsy did turn to her with a great laugh:

'It's the one pleasure of my life to have your hands on me,' he gibed. 'Give me another puck now, and a hard one, the way I'll feel you well.'

The woman lifted her ash-plant threateningly and crouched towards him, but the look on his face was such that she let her hand fall again.

'You're full of fun,' said Patsy, 'and you always were, but we're going to be the great friends from now on, yourself and myself and the man with the stick; we'll be going by short cuts everywhere in the world, and having a gay time.'

'We're not going with you, Padraig,' said the woman, 'and whatever road you are taking this day, the man and myself will be going another road.'

'Whoo!' said Patsy, 'there are roads everywhere, so you're all right, and there are men on every one of the roads.'

CHAPTER XIV

WHILE this conversation had been taking place the others stood in a grave semicircle, and listened intently to their words.

Caeltia, regarding the sky, intervened:

'The rain will be here in a minute, so we had better walk on and look for shelter.'

Mac Cann detached his heavy regard from Eileen Ni Cooley, and swept the sky and the horizon.

'That is so,' said he. 'Let us go ahead now for we've had our talk, and we are all satisfied.

'There is a broken-down house stuck up a bohereen,' he continued. 'It's only a few perches up this road, for I remember passing the place the last time I was this way; that place will give us shelter while the rain spills.'

He turned his stubborn face to the woman:

'You can come with us if you like, and you can stay where you are if you like, or you can go to the devil,' and, saying so, he tramped after his daughter.

The woman had just caught sight of Art the cherub, and was regarding him with her steady eyes.

'Whoo!' said she, 'I'm not the one to be frightened, and I never was, so let us all go along and talk about our sins in the wet weather.'

They started anew on the road, Patsy's company in advance, and behind marched the woman and the man and Art the cherub.

The sun had disappeared; wild clouds were piling themselves in rugged hills along the sky, and the world was growing dull and chill. Against the grey atmosphere Art's face was in profile, an outline sharp and calm and beautiful.

Eileen Ni Cooley was regarding him curiously as they walked together, and the strange man, with a wry smile on his lips, was regarding her with a like curiosity.

She pointed towards Patsy Mac Cann, who was tramping vigorously a dozen yards ahead.

'Young boy,' said she, 'where did you pick up with the man yonder, for the pair of you don't look matched?'

Art had his hands in his pockets; he turned and looked at her tranquilly.

'Where did you pick up with that man'—he nodded towards her companion—'and where did the man pick up with you, for you don't looked matched either?'

'We're not,' said the woman quickly; 'we're not matched a bit. That man and myself do be quarrelling all day and all night, and threatening to walk away from each other every minute of the time.'

The man stared at her.

'Is that how it is with us?' said he.

'It is,' said she to Art—'that's the way it is with us, honey. The man and myself have no love for each other now, and we never had.'

The man halted suddenly; he changed the cudgel to his left hand and thrust out his right hand to her.

'Put your own hand there,' said he, 'and shake it well, and then be going along your road.'

'What are you talking about?' said she.

He replied, frowning sternly from his wild eyes:

'I wouldn't hold the grace of God if I saw it slipping from me, so put your hand into my hand and go along your road.'

Eileen Ni Cooley put her hand into his with some awkwardness and turned away her head.

'There it is for you,' said she.

Then the man turned about and flapped quickly along the

path they had already travelled; his cudgel beat the ground with a sharp noise, and he did not once look back.

Before he had taken an hundred paces the rain came, a fine, noiseless drizzle.

'It will be heavy in a minute,' said the woman, 'let us run after the cart.'

With a quick movement she tucked her shawl about her head and shoulders and started to run, and Art went after her in alternate long hops of each foot.

They had reached a narrow path running diagonally from the main road.

'Up this way,' shouted Patsy, and the company trooped after him, leaving the ass and cart to the storm.

Two minutes' distance up the road stood a small, dismantled house. There was a black gape where the window had been, and there were holes in the walls. In these holes grass and weeds were waving, as they were along the window-ledge. The roof was covered with a rusty thatch and there were red poppies growing on that.

Patsy climbed through the low window-space, and the others climbed in after him.

CHAPTER XV

INSIDE the house was an earthen floor, four walls, and plenty of air. There were breezes blowing in the empty house, for from whatever direction a wind might come it found entrance there. There were stones lying everywhere on the floor; some of them had dropped from the walls, but most had been jerked through the window by passing children. There were spiders' webs in that house; the roof was covered with them, and the walls were covered with them too. It was a dusty house, and when it would be wet enough it would be a muddy house, and it was musty with disuse and desolation.

But the company did not care anything about dust or stones or spiders. They kicked the stones aside and sat on the floor in the most sheltered part of the place where there had once been a fireplace, and if a spider walked on any of them it was permitted.

Patsy produced a clay pipe and lit it, and Caeltia took a silver-mounted briar from his pocket and he lit that and smoked it.

Outside the rain suddenly began to fall with a low noise and the room grew dark. Within there was a brooding quietness, for none of the people spoke; they were all waiting for each other to speak.

Indeed, they had all been agitated when they came in, for the wrung face of Patsy and the savage eyes of Eileen Ni Cooley had whipped their blood. Tragedy had sounded her warning note on the air, and they were each waiting to see had they a part in the play.

But the sudden change of atmosphere wrought like a foreign chemical in their blood, the sound of the falling rain dulled their spirits, the must of that sleeping house went to their brains like an opiate, and the silence of the place folded them about, compelling them to a similar quietude.

We are imitative beings; we respond to the tone and colour of our environment almost against ourselves and still have our links with the chameleon and the moth; the sunset sheds its radiant peace upon us and we are content; the silent mountain-top lays a finger on our lips and we talk in whispers; the clouds lend us of their gaiety and we rejoice. So for a few moments they sat wrestling with the dull ghosts of that broken house, the mournful phantasms that were not dead long enough to be happy, for death is sorrowful at first and for a long time, but afterwards the dead are contented and learn to shape themselves anew.

Patsy, drawing on his pipe, looked around the people:

'Eh!' he exclaimed with heavy joviality, 'where has the man got to, the man with the big stick? If he's shy let him come in, and if he's angry let him come in too.'

Eileen Ni Cooley was sitting close beside Art. She had let her shawl droop from her head, and her hair was showing through the dusk like a torch.

'The man has gone away, Padraig,' said she; 'he got tired of the company, and he's gone travelling towards his own friends.'

Patsy regarded her with shining eyes. The must of the house was no longer in his nostrils; the silence lifted from him at a bound.

'You are telling me a fine story, Eileen,' said he; 'tell me this too, did the man go away of his own will, or did you send him away?'

'It was a bit of both, Padraig.'

'The time to get good news,' said Patsy, 'is when it's raining, and that is good news, and it's raining now.'

'News need not be good or bad, but only news,' she replied, 'and we will leave it at that.'

74

Caeltia spoke to her:

'Do you have a good life going by yourself about the country and making acquaintances where you please?'

'I have the life I like,' she answered, 'and whether it's good or bad doesn't matter.'

'Tell me the reason you never let himself make love to you when he wants to make it?'

'He is a domineering man,' said she, 'and I am a proud woman, and we would never give in to each other. When one of us would want to do a thing the other one wouldn't do it, and there would be no living between us. If I said black he would say white, and if he said yes I would say no, and that's how we are.'

'He has a great love for you.'

'He has a great hate for me. He loves me the way a dog loves bones, and in a little while he'd kill me in a lonely place with his hands to see what I would look like and I dying.'

She turned her face to Mac Cann:

'That's the kind of man you are to me, Padraig, although you're different to other people.'

'I am not that sort of man, but it's yourself is like that. I tell you that if I took a woman with me I'd be staunch to her the way I was with the mother of the girl there, and if you were to come with me you wouldn't have any complaint from now on.'

'I know every thing I'm talking about,' she replied sternly, 'and I won't go with you, but I'll go with the young man here beside me.'

With the words she put her hand on Art's arm and kept it there.

Mary Mac Cann straightened up where she was sitting and became deeply interested.

Art turned and burst into a laugh as he looked critically at Eileen.

'I will not go with you,' said he. 'I don't care for you a bit.'

75

She gave a hard smile and removed her hand from his arm.

'It's all the worse for me,' said she, 'and it's small harm to you, young boy.'

'That's a new answer for yourself,' said Patsy, grinning savagely.

'It is, and it's a new day for me, and a poor day, for it's the first day of my old age.'

'You'll die in a ditch,' cried Patsy, 'you'll die in a ditch like an old mare with a broken leg.'

'I will,' she snarled, 'when the time comes, but you'll never have the killing of me, Padraig.'

Finaun was sitting beside Mary with her hand in his, but she snatched her hand away and flared so fiercely upon Eileen that the woman looked up.

'Don't be angry with me, Mary,' said she; 'I never did you any harm yet and I'll never be able to do it now, for there are years between us, and they're going to break my back.'

Finaun was speaking, more, it seemed, to himself than to the company. He combed his white beard with his hand as he spoke, and they all looked at him.

'He is talking in his sleep,' said Eileen pensively, 'and he an old man, and a nice old man.'

'My father,' said Caeltia, in an apologetic voice; 'there is no need to tell about that.'

'There is every need, my beloved,' replied Finaun, with his slow smile.

'I would rather you did not,' murmured Caeltia, lifting his hand a little.

'I ask your permission, my son,' said Finaun gently.

Caeltia spread out his open palms and dropped them again.

'Whatever you wish to do is good, my father,' and, with a slight blush, he slid the pipe into his pocket.

Finaun turned to Eileen Ni Cooley:

'I will tell you a story,' said he.

'Sure,' said Eileen, 'I'd love to hear you, and I could listen to a story for a day and a night.'

Mac Cann pulled solemnly at his pipe and regarded Finaun, who was looking at him peacefully from a corner.

'You're full of fun,' said he to the archangel.

CHAPTER XVI

SAID Finaun:

'While generation succeeds generation a man has to fight the same fight. At the end he wins, and he never has to fight that battle again, and then he is ready for Paradise.

'Every man from the beginning has one enemy from whom he can never escape, and the story of his lives is the story of his battles with that enemy whom he must draw into his own being before he can himself attain to real being, for an enemy can never be crushed, but every enemy can be won.

'Long before the foundations of this world were laid, when the voice was heard and the army of the voice went through the darkness, two people came into being with the universe that was their shell. They lived through myriad existences, knowing star after star grow hot and cold in the broad sky, and they hated each other through the changing of the stars and the ebbing and flooding of their lives.

'At a time this one of them would be a woman and that other would be a man, and again in due period the one that had been a woman would be a man and the other would be a woman, that their battle might be joined in the intimacy which can only come through difference and the distance that is attraction.

'No one can say which of these did most harm to the other; no one can say which was the most ruthless, the most merciless, for they were born, as all enemies are, equal in being and in power.

'Through their lives they had many names and they lived in many lands, but their names in eternity were Finaun Mac

Dea and Caeltia Mac Dea, and when the time comes, their name will be Mac Dea and nothing else: then they will become one in each other, and one in Infinite Greatness, and one in the unending life of Eternity which is God; but still, in world under world, in star under flaming star, they pursue each other with a hate which is slowly changing into love.

'It was not on earth, nor in any planet, that the beginning of love came to these two, it was in the hell that they had fashioned for themselves in terror and lust and cruelty. For, as they sat among their demons, a seed germinated in the soul of one, the seed of knowledge which is the parent of love and the parent of every terrible and beautiful thing in the worlds and the heavens.

'While that one looked on his companion, writhing like himself in torment, he grew conscious, and although he looked at the other with fury it was with a new fury, for with it came contempt, and they were no longer equal in power or in hate.

'Now, for the first time, that one in whom knowledge had been born desired to escape from his companion; he wished to get away so that he might never behold that enemy again; suddenly the other appeared to him hideous as a toad that couches in slime and spits his poison at random, but he could not escape, and he could never escape.

'As that one increased in knowledge so he increased in cruelty and power, so his lust became terrible, for now there was fear in his contempt because he could never escape. Many a time they fled from one another, but always, and however they fled, it was towards each other their steps were directed. At the feast, in the camp, and in the wilderness they found themselves and undertook anew the quarrel which was their blood and their being.

'And that other in whom knowledge had not awakened— He raged like a beast; he thought in blood and fever; his brains were his teeth and the nails of his hands. Cunning came creepingly to his aid against knowledge; he lay in wait for his enemy in gloomy places; he spread snares for him in the darkness and baited traps. He feigned humility to get closer to his vengeance, but he could not combat knowledge.

'Time and again he became the slave of that other, and as slave and master their battle was savagely joined, until at last knowledge stirred also in that mind and he grew conscious.

'Then the age-long enmity drew to its change. For him there was no contempt possible, the other was older than he and wiser, for to be wise is to be old; there was no vantage for contempt, but envy sharpened his sword, it salted his anger, and they fought anew and unceasingly.

'But now their hands were not seeking each other's throats with such frank urgency; they fought subterraneously, with smiles and polite words and decent observances, but they did not cease for an instant to strive, and never did they forsake an advantage or lift up the one that had fallen.

'Again the change: and now they battled not in the name of hate but under the holy superscription of love; again and again, life after life, they harried and ruined each other; their desire for one another was a madness, and in that desire they warred more bitterly than before. They blasted each other's lives, they dashed their honour to the mud, they slew one another. Than this none of their battles had been so terrible. Here there was no let, no respite even for an instant. They knew each other with that superficial knowledge which seems so clear although it shows no more than the scum floating upon existence; they knew the scumminess of each other and exhausted to the dregs their abundant evil until of evil they could learn no further, and their lives, alternating in a fierce energy and a miserable weariness, came towards but could not come to stagnation.

'The horizon vanished from them; there were irons on the

feet of the winds; the sun peered from a hood through a mask and life was one room wherein dull voices droned dully, wherein something was for ever uttered and nothing was said, where hands were for ever lifted and nothing was done, where the mind smouldered and flared to lightning and no thought came from the spark.

'They had reached an end, and it was a precipice down which they must spin giddily to the murk, or else shape wings for themselves and soar from that completion, for completion is a consciousness, and once again they were powerfully aware of themselves. They were vice-conscious, and virtue did not abide in their minds than as a dream which was an illusion and a lie.

'Then—and this too was long ago! how long! When the moon was young; when she gathered rosy clouds about her evening and sang at noon from bush and mountain-ledge; when she folded her breasts in dewy darkness and awakened with cries of joy to the sun; then she tended her flowers in the vale; she drove her kine to deep pasture; she sang to her multitudes of increase and happiness while her feet went in the furrow with the plough and her hand guided the sickle and the sheaf. Great love didst thou give when thou wast a mother, O Beautiful! who art now white as silver and hath ice upon thine ancient head.

'Again they lived and were wed.

'Which of them was which in that sad pilgrimage it is not now possible to know. Memory faints at the long tale of it, and they were so intermingled, so alike through all their difference, that they were becoming one in the great memory. Again they took up the time-long burden, and again desire drew them wildly to the embrace which was much repugnance and very little love. So, behold these two, a man and a woman, walking through the pleasant light, taking each other's hands in a kindness that had no roots, speaking words of affection that their souls groaned the lie to.

'The woman was fair—she was fair as one star that shines on the void and is not abashed before immensity; she was beautiful as a green tree by a pool that bows peacefully to the sun; she was lovely as a field of mild corn waving to the wind in one slow movement. Together they plumbed their desire and found wickedness glooming at the bottom, and they were conscious of themselves and of all evil.

'There was a demon in the pit that they had digged, and always, when they founded anew their hell, he tormented them; he was the accumulation of their evil; age after age they re-created him until he showed gigantic and terrible as a storm, and as they lusted after each other so he lusted after them.

'On a time that Misery shaped itself as a man and came privily to the woman while she walked under heavy apple boughs in a garden. Their feet went to and fro closely together in the grass and their voices communed together, until one day the woman cried bitterly that there were no wings, and with the Spectre she leaped forthright to the chasm and went down shrieking a laughter that was woe. There she found herself and her demon and was the concubine of that one; and there, in the gulf and chasm of evil, she conjured virtue to her tortured soul and stole energy from the demon.

'She sat among the rocks of her place.

'Old Misery beside her laughed his laugh, and while she looked at him her eyes went backwards in her head, and when she looked again she saw differently, for in that space knowledge had put forth a bud and a blossom and she looked through knowledge. She saw herself and the demon and the man, and she prayed to the demon. As she prayed she gathered small blue flowers that peered sparsely among the crags, and she made a chaplet of these. She wove them with tears and sighs, and when the chaplet was made she put it to the demon's hand, praying him to bear it to the man.

'He did that for her because he loved to laugh at their trouble, and he divined laughter for his iron chaps.

'So the demon came terribly to the man as he walked under the swaying and lifting of green boughs in the long grass of an orchard, and he put the chaplet in the man's hand saying:

' "My concubine, your beloved, sends a greeting to you with her love and this garland of blue flowers which she has woven with her two hands in hell."

'The man, looking on these flowers, felt his heart move within him like water.

' "Bring her to me," said he to the demon.

' "I will not do so," replied the Misery.

'And, suddenly, the man leaped on the Spectre. He locked his arms about that cold neck, and clung furiously with his knees.

' "Then I will go to her with you," said he.

'And together they went headlong down the pit, and as they fell they battled frightfully in the dark pitch.'

CHAPTER XVII

MAC CANN was asleep, but when Finaun's voice ceased he awakened and stretched himself with a loud yawn.

'I didn't hear a word of that story,' said he.

'I heard it,' said Eileen Ni Cooley; 'it was a good story.'

'What was it about?'

'I don't know,' she replied.

'Do you know what it was about, Mary?'

'I do not, for I was thinking about other things at the time.'

Finaun took her hand.

'There was no need for any of you to know what that story was about, excepting you only'; and he looked very kindly at Eileen Ni Cooley.

'I listened to it,' said she; 'and it was a good story. I know what it was about, but I would not know how to tell what it was about.'

'It must have been the queer yarn,' said Patsy regretfully; 'I wish I hadn't gone to sleep.'

'I was awake for you,' said Caeltia.

'What's the use of that?' said Patsy testily.

It was still raining.

The day was far advanced and evening was spinning her dull webs athwart the sky. Already in the broken house the light had diminished to a brown gloom, and their faces looked watchful and pale to each other as they crouched on the earthen floor. Silence was again seizing on them, and each person's eyes were focussing on some object or point on the wall or the floor as their thoughts began to hold them.

Mac Cann roused himself.

'We are here for the night; that rain won't stop as long as there's a drop left in its can.'

Mary bestirred herself also.

'I'll slip down to the cart and bring back whatever food is in it. I left everything covered and I don't think they'll be too wet.'

'Do that,' said her father.

'There's a big bottle rolled up in a sack,' he continued; 'it's in a bucket at the front of the cart by the right shaft, and there's a little sup of whisky in the big bottle.'

'I'll bring that too.'

'You're a good girl,' said he.

'What will I do with the ass this night?' said Mary.

'Hit him a kick,' said her father.

CHAPTER XVIII

THE ass stood quietly where he had been left.

Rain was pouring from him as though he were the father of rivers and supplied the world with running water. It dashed off his flanks; it leaped down his tail; it foamed over his forehead to his nose, and hit the ground from there with a thump.

'I'm very wet,' said the ass to himself, 'and I wish I wasn't.'

His eyes were fixed on a brown stone that had a knob on its back. Every drop of rain that hit the stone jumped twice and then spattered to the ground. After a moment he spoke to himself again:

'I don't care whether it stops raining or not, for I can't be any wetter than I am, however it goes.'

Having said this, he dismissed the weather and settled himself to think. He hung his head slightly and fixed his eyes afar off, and he stared distantly like that without seeing anything while he gathered and revolved his thoughts.

The first thing he thought about was carrots.

He thought of their shape, their colour, and the way they looked in a bucket. Some would have the thick end stuck up, and some would have the other end stuck up, and there were always bits of clay sticking to one end or the other. Some would be lying on their sides as though they had slipped quietly to sleep, and some would be standing in a slanting way as though they were leaning their backs against a wall and couldn't make up their minds what to do next. But, however they looked in the bucket, they all tasted alike, and they all tasted well. They are a companionable food; they make a pleasant, crunching noise when they are bitten, and so, when one is eating carrots, one can listen to the sound of one's eating and make a story from it.

Thistles make a swishing noise when they are bitten; they have their taste.

Grass does not make any noise at all; it slips dumbly to the sepulchre, and makes no sign.

Bread makes no sound when it is eaten by an ass; it has an interesting taste, and it clings about one's teeth for a long time.

Apples have a good smell and a joyful crunch, but the taste of sugar lasts longer in the mouth, and can be remembered for longer than anything else; it has a short, sharp crunch that is like a curse, and instantly it blesses you with the taste of it.

Hay can be eaten in great mouthfuls. It has a chip and a crack at the first bite, and then it says no more. It sticks out of one's mouth like whiskers, and you can watch it with your eye while it moves to and fro according as your mouth moves. It is a friendly food, and very good for the hungry.

Oats are not a food; they are a great blessing; they are a debauch; they make you proud, so that you want to kick the front out of a cart, and climb a tree, and bite a cow, and chase chickens.

Mary came running and unyoked him from the cart. She embraced him on the streaming nose. 'You poor thing, you!' said she, and she took a large paper bag from the cart and held it to his muzzle. There was soft sugar in the bag, and half a pound of it clove to his tongue at the first lick.

As she went back to the house with the bundle of food the ass regarded her.

'You are a good girl,' said the ass.

He shook himself and dissipated his thoughts; then he trotted briskly here and there on the path to see if there was anything worth looking for.

CHAPTER XIX

THEY shared the food: there was little of it, and some of it was wet; but they each had a piece of bread, a knuckle of cheese, and three cold potatoes.

Mary said there was something wrong with her, and she passed two of her cold potatoes to the cherub Art, who ate them easily.

'I wish you had given them to me,' said her father.

'I'll give you one of mine,' said Eileen Ni Cooley, and she thrust one across to him.

Mac Cann pushed it entire into his mouth, and ate it as one who eats in a trance: he stared at Eileen.

'Why did you give me your potato?' said he.

Eileen blushed until not a single freckle in her face was visible.

'I don't know,' she answered.

'You don't seem to know anything at all this day,' he complained. 'You're full of fun,' said he.

He lit his pipe, and, after pulling for a while at it, he handed it to the woman.

'Take a draw at that pipe,' he commanded, 'and let us be decent with each other.'

Eileen Ni Cooley did take a draw at the pipe, but she handed it back soon.

'I never was much at the smoking,' said she.

Caeltia had his pipe going at full blast. He was leaning against the wall with his eyes half closed, and was thinking deeply between puffs.

Finaun had a good grip on Mary's hair, which he was methodically plaiting and unloosening again. He was sunken in reverie.

Mary was peeping from beneath her lids at Art, and was at the same time watching everybody else to see that she was not observed.

Art was whistling to himself in a low tone, and he was looking fixedly at a spider.

The spider was hauling on a loose rope of his tent, and he was very leisurely. One would have thought that he was smoking also.

'What did you have for dinner?' said Art to the spider.

'Nothing, sir, but a little, thin wisp of a young fly,' said the spider.

He was a thick-set, heavy kind of spider, and he seemed to be middle-aged, and resigned to it.

'That is all I had myself,' said Art. 'Are the times bad with you now, or are they middling?'

'Not so bad, glory be to God! The flies do wander in through the holes, and when they come from the light out-side to the darkness in here, sir, we catch them on the wall, and we crunch their bones.'

'Do they like that?'

'They do not, sir, but we do. The lad with the stout, hairy legs, down there beside your elbow, caught a blue-bottle yesterday; there was eating on that fellow I tell you, and he's not all eaten yet, but that spider is always lucky, barring the day he caught the wasp.'

'That was a thing he didn't like?' queried Art.

'Don't mention it to him, sir, he doesn't care to talk about it.'

'What way are you going to fasten up your rope?' said Art.

'I'll put a spit on the end of it, and then I'll thump it with my head to make it stick.'

'Well, good luck to yourself.'

'Good luck to your honour.'

*

Said Patsy to Caeltia, pointing to Finaun:

'What does he be thinking about when he gets into them fits?'

'He does be talking to the hierarchy,' replied Caeltia.

'And who are themselves?'

'They are the poeple in charge of this world.'

'Is it the kings and the queens and the Holy Pope?'

'No, they are different kinds of people.'

Patsy yawned.

'What does he be talking to them about?'

'Every kind of thing,' replied Caeltia, and yawned also. 'They are asking him for advice now.'

'What is he saying?'

'He is talking about love,' said Caeltia.

'He is always talking about that,' said Patsy.

'And,' said Caeltia, 'he is talking about knowledge.'

'It's another word of his.'

'And he is saying that love and knowledge are the same thing.'

'I wouldn't put it past him,' said Patsy.

For he was in a bad temper. Either the close confinement, or the dull weather, or the presence of Eileen Ni Cooley, or all of these had made him savage.

He arose and began striding through the narrow room, kicking stones from one side of the place to the other and glooming fiercely at everybody. Twice he halted before Eileen Ni Cooley, staring at her, and twice, without a word said, he resumed his marching.

Suddenly he leaned his back against the wall facing her, and shouted:

'Well, Eileen a grah, the man went away from you, the man with the big stick and the lengthy feet. Ah! that's a man you'd be crying out for and you all by yourself in the night.'

91

'He was a good man,' said Eileen; 'there was no harm in that man, Padraig.'

'Maybe he used to be putting his two arms around you now and then beside a hedge and giving you long kisses on the mouth?'

'He used to be doing that.'

'Aye did he, indeed, and he wasn't the first man to do that, Eileen.'

'Maybe you're right, Padraig.'

'Nor the twenty-first.'

'You've got me here in the house, Padraig, and the people around us are your own friends.'

Caeltia also had arisen to his feet and was staring morosely at Eileen. Suddenly he leaped to her, wrenched the shawl from her head with a wide gesture, and gripped her throat between his hands; as her head touched the ground she gasped, and then, and just as suddenly, he released her. He stood up looking wildly at Patsy, who stared back at him grinning like a madman, then he stumbled across to Finaun and took his hands between his own.

'You must not hurt me, my dear,' said Finaun, smiling gravely at him.

Mary had leaped to Art, whose arm she took, and they backed to the end of the room.

Eileen stood up; she arranged her dress and wrapped the shawl about her head again; she gazed fearlessly at Mac Cann.

'The house is full of your friends, Padraig, and there's nobody here with me at all; there's no man could want better than that for himself.'

Patsy's voice was hoarse:

'You're looking for fight?'

'I'm looking for whatever is coming,' said replied steadily.

'I'm coming then,' he roared, and he strode to her. He

lifted his hands above his head, and brought them down so heavily on her shoulders that she staggered.

'Here I am,' said he, staring into her face.

She closed her eyes.

'I knew it wasn't love you wanted, Padraig; it was murder you wanted, and you have your wish.'

She was swaying under his weight as she spoke; her knees were giving beneath her.

'Eileen,' said Patsy, in a small voice, 'I'm going to tumble; I can't hold myself up, Eileen; my knees are giving way under me, and I've only got my arms round your neck.'

She opened her eyes and saw him sagging against her, with his eyes half closed and his face gone white.

'Sure, Padraig!' said she.

She flung her arms about his body and lifted him, but the weight was too much, and he went down.

She crouched by him on the floor, hugging his head against her breast.

'Sure, listen to me, Padraig; I never did like any one in the world but yourself; there wasn't a man of them all was more to me than a blast of wind; you were the one I liked always. Listen to me now, Padraig. Don't I be wanting you day and night, and saying prayers to you in the darkness and crying out in the dawn; my heart is sore for you, so it is: there's a twist in us, O my dear. Don't you be minding the men; whatever they did it was nothing, it was nothing more than beasts playing in a field and not caring anything. We are beside one another for a minute now. When I would put my hand on my breast in the middle of a laugh it was you I was touching, and I do never stop thinking of you in any place under the sky.'

They were kissing each other like lost souls; they babbled and clung to each other; they thrust one another's head back to stare at it, and pursued the head with their violent lips.

*

93

It was a time before they all got to sleep that night, but they did sleep at the end of it.

They stretched in the darkness with their eyes closed, and the night folded them around, separating each one from his fellow, and putting on each the enchantment of silence and blindness. They were no longer together although they were lying but a few inches apart; there was only the darkness that had no inches to it; the darkness that has no beginning and no end; that appears and disappears, calling hush as it comes and goes, and holding peace and terror in either invisible hand; there was no silver moon in the sky and no sparkle of white stars; there was only darkness and silence and the steady hushing of the rain.

When he awoke in the morning Mac Cann rolled urgently on his elbow, and stared to where Eileen Ni Cooley had stretched herself for sleep—but she was not there, she was not anywhere.

He shouted, and the company sprang to their feet.

'She got out through the window,' he roared.

'The devil damn the soul of her,' said he.

CHAPTER XX

THEY continued their travels.

It would be more correct to say they continued their search for food, for that in reality was the objective of each day's journeying.

Moving thus, day by day, taking practically any road that presented itself, they had wandered easily through rugged, beautiful Donegal down into Connaught. They had camped on the slopes of rough mountains, slept peacefully in deep valleys that wound round and round like a corkscrew, traversed for weeks in Connemara by the clamorous sea where they lived sumptuously on fish, and then they struck to the inland plains again, and away by curving paths to the County Kerry.

At times Mac Cann got work to do—to mend a kettle that had a little hole in it, to stick a handle on a pot, to stiffen the last days of a bucket that was already long past its labour; and he did these jobs sitting in the sunlight on dusty roads, and if he did not do them Mary did them for him, while he observed her critically and explained both to her and to his company the mystery of the tinker's craft.

'There's a great deal,' he would say, 'in the twist of the hand.'

And again, but this usually to Art when that cherub tried his skill on a rusty pot:

'You'll never make a good tinker unless you've got a hand on you. Keep your feet in your boots and get to work with your fingers.'

And sometimes he would nod contentedly at Mary and say:

'There's a girl with real hands on her that aren't feet.'

Hands represented to him whatever of praiseworthy might be spoken of by a man, but feet were in his opinion rightly covered, and ought not to be discovered except in minatory conversation. One ran on them! Well, it was a dog's trade, or a donkey's; but hands! he expanded to that subject, and could loose thereon a gale of praise that would blow all other conversation across the border.

They set their camp among roaring fairs where every kind of wild man and woman yelled salutation at Patsy and his daughter, and howled remembrance of ten and twenty-year-old follies, and plunged into drink with the savage alacrity of those to whom despair is a fairer brother than hope; and with some of these people the next day's journey would be shared, rioting and screaming on the lonely roads, and these people also the angels observed and were friendly with.

One morning they were pacing on their journey. The eyes of the little troop were actively scanning the fields on either hand. They were all hungry, for they had eaten nothing since the previous mid-day. But these fields were barren of food. Great stretches of grass extended away to either horizon, and there was nothing here that could be eaten except by the donkey.

As they went they saw a man sitting on a raised bank. His arms were folded; he had a straw in his mouth; there was a broad grin on his red face; a battered hat was thrust far back on his head, and from beneath this a brush of stiff hair poked in any direction like an ill-tied bundle of black wire.

Mac Cann stared at that red joviality.

'There's a man,' said he to Caeltia, 'that hasn't got a care in the world.'

'It must be very bad for him,' commented Caeltia.

'Holloa, mister,' cried Patsy heartily, 'how's everything?'

'Everything's fine,' beamed the man; 'how's yourself?'

'We're holding up, glory be to God!'

'That's the way.'

He waved his hand against the horizon.

'There's weather for you,' and he spoke with the proud humility of one who had made that weather, but would not boast. His eye was steady on Mac Cann.

'I've got a hunger on me that's worth feeding, mister.'

'We've all got that,' replied Patsy, 'and there's nothing in the cart barring its timbers. I'm keeping an eye out tho', and maybe we'll trip over a side of bacon in the middle of the road, or a neat little patch of potatoes in the next field, and it full of the flowery boyoes.'

'There's a field a mile up this road,' said the man, 'and everything you could talk about is in that field.'

'Do you tell me!' said Patsy briskly.

'I do: every kind of thing is in that field, and there's rabbits at the foot of the hill beyond it.'

'I used to have a good shot with a stone,' said Patsy.

'Mary,' he continued, 'when we come to the field let yourself and Art gather up the potatoes while Caeltia and myself take stones in our hands to kill the rabbits.'

'I'm coming along with you,' said the man, 'and I'll get my share.'

'You can do that,' said Patsy.

The man scrambled down the bank. There was something between his knees of which he was very careful.

'What sort of a thing is that?' said Mary.

'It's a concertina, and I do play tunes on it before the houses, and that's how I make my money.'

'The musiciner will give us a tune after we get a feed,' said Patsy.

'Sure enough,' said the man.

Art stretched out his hand.

'Let me have a look at the musical instrument,' said he.

The man handed it to him and fell into pace beside Patsy and Caeltia. Mary and Finaun were going as usual one on

99

either side of the ass, and the three of them returned to their interrupted conversation. Every dozen paces Finaun would lean to the border of the road and pluck a fist-full of prime grass or a thistle or a clutch of chickweed, and he would put these to the ass's mouth.

Patsy was eyeing the man.

'What's your name, mister?' said he.

'I was known as Old Carolan, but now the people call me Billy the Music.'

'How is it that I never met you before?'

'I'm from Connemara.'

'I know every cow-track and bohereen in Connemara, and I know every road in Donegal and Kerry, and I know everybody that's on them roads, but I don't know you, mister.'

The man laughed at him.

'I'm not long on the roads, so how could you know me? What are you called yourself?'

'I'm called Padraig Mac Cann.'

'I know you well, for you stole a hen and a pair of boots off me ten months ago when I lived in a house.'

'Do you tell me?' said Mac Cann.

'I do; and I never grudged them to you, for that was the day that everything happened to me.'

Mac Cann was searching his head to find from whom he had stolen a hen and a pair of boots at the one time.

'Well, glory be to God!' he cried. 'Isn't it the queer world! Are you old Carolan the miserly man of Temple Cahill?'

The man laughed and nodded.

'I used to be him, but now I'm Billy the Music, and there's my instrument under the boy's oxter.'

Patsy stared at him.

'And where's the house and the cattle, and the hundred acres of grass land and glebe, and the wife that people said you used to starve the stomach out of?'

'Faith, I don't know where they are, and I don't care either,' and he shook with the laughter as he said it.

'And your sister that killed herself climbing out of a high window on a windy night to search for food among the neighbours?'

'She's dead still,' said the man, and he doubled up with glee.

'I declare,' said Patsy, 'that it's the end of the world.'

The man broke on his eloquence with a pointed finger.

'There's the field I was telling you about, and it's weighty to the ribs with potatoes and turnips.'

Patsy turned to his daughter.

'Gather in the potatoes; don't take them all from the one place, but take them from here and there the way they won't be missed, and then go along the road with the cart for twenty minutes and be cooking them. Myself and Caeltia will catch up on you in a little time and we'll bring good meat with us.'

Caeltia and he moved to the right where a gentle hill rose against the sky. The hill was thickly wooded, massive clumps of trees were dotted every little distance, and through these one could see quiet, green spaces drowsing in the sun.

When they came to the fringing trees Patsy directed his companion to go among them some little distance, and then to charge here and there, slashing against the trees and the ground with a stick.

Caeltia did that, and at the end of a quarter of an hour Patsy had three rabbits stretched under his hand.

That's good enough,' he called; 'we'll go on now after the people.'

They stowed the rabbits under their coats and took the road.

They soon caught on their companions. The cart was drawn to the side of the road, at a little distance the ass was

101

browsing, and Mary had a fire going in the brazier and the potatoes ready for the pot.

Patsy tossed the rabbits to her.

'There you are, my girl,' said he, and, with Caeltia, he sank down on the grassy margin of the road and drew out his pipe.

The strange man was sitting beside Art, to whom he was explaining the mechanism of a concertina.

'While we are waiting,' said Patsy to him, 'you can tell us all the news; tell us what happened to the land and what you're doing on the road; and there is a bit of twist to put in your pipe so that you'll talk well.'

Mary broke in:

'Wait a minute now for I want to hear that story; let yourself help me over with the brazier and we can all sit together.'

There was a handle to the bucket, and through this they put a long stick and lifted all bodily to the butt of the hedge.

'Now we can sit together,' said Mary, 'and I can be cooking the food and listening to the story at the same time.'

'I'd sooner give you a tune on the concertina,' said Billy the Music.

'You can do that afterwards,' replied Patsy.

CHAPTER XXI

'I'LL tell you the story,' said Billy the Music, 'and here it is:

'A year ago I had a farm in the valley. The sun shone into it, and the wind didn't blow into it for it was well sheltered, and the crops that I used to take off that land would astonish you.

'I had twenty head of cattle eating the grass, and they used to get fat quick, and they used to give good milk into the bargain. I had cocks and hens for the eggs and the market, and there was a good many folk would have been glad to get my farm.

'There were ten men always working on the place, but at harvest-time there would be a lot more, and I used to make them work too. Myself and my son and my wife's brother (a lout, that fellow!) used to run after the men, but it was hard to keep up with them for they were great schemers. They tried to do as little work as ever they were able, and they tried to get as much money out of me as they could manage. But I was up to them lads, and it's mighty little they got out of me without giving twice as much for it.

'Bit by bit I weeded out the men until at last I only had the ones I wanted, the tried and trusty men. They were a poor lot, and they didn't dare to look back at me when I looked at them; but they were able to work, and that is all I wanted them to do, and I saw that they did it.

'As I'm sitting beside you on this bank to-day I'm wondering why I took all the trouble I did take, and what, in the name of this and that, I expected to get out of it all. I usen't go to bed until twelve o'clock at night, and I would be up in the dawn before the birds. Five o'clock in the morning never saw me stretching in the warm bed, and every day I would root the men out of their sleep; often enough I had to throw them out of bed, for there wasn't a man of them but would have slept rings round the clock if he got the chance.

'Of course I knew that they didn't want to work for me, and that, bating the hunger, they'd have seen me far enough before they'd lift a hand for my good; but I had them by the hasp, for as long as men have to eat, any man with the food can make them do whatever he wants them to do; wouldn't they stand on their heads for twelve hours a day if you gave them wages? Aye would they, and eighteen hours if you held them to it.

'I had the idea too that they were trying to rob me, and maybe they were. It doesn't seem to matter now whether they robbed me or not, for I give you my word that the man who wants to rob me to-day is welcome to all he can get and more if I had it.'

'Faith, you're the kind man!' said Patsy.

'Let that be,' said Billy the Music.

'The secret of the thing was that I loved money, hard money, gold and silver pieces, and pieces of copper. I liked it better than the people who were round me. I liked it better than the cattle and the crops. I liked it better than I liked myself, and isn't that the queer thing? I put up with the silliest ways for it, and I lived upside down and inside out for it. I tell you I would have done anything just to get money, and when I paid the men for their labour I grudged them every penny that they took from me.

'It did seem to me that in taking my metal they were surely and openly robbing me and laughing at me as they did it. I saw no reason why they shouldn't have worked for me for nothing, and if they had I would have grudged them the food they ate and the time they lost in sleeping, and that's another queer thing, mind you!'

'If one of them men,' said Patsy solemnly, 'had the spunk

of a wandering goat or a mangy dog he'd have taken a graipe to yourself, mister, and he'd have picked your soul out of your body and slung it on a dung-heap.'

'Don't be thinking,' replied the other, 'that men are courageous and fiery animals, for they're not, and every person that pays wages to men knows well that they're as timid as sheep and twice as timid. Let me tell you too that all the trouble wasn't on their side; I had a share of it and a big share.'

Mac Cann interrupted solemnly:

'That's what the fox told the goose when the goose said that the teeth hurted him. "Look at the trouble I had to catch you," said the fox.'

'We won't mind that,' said Billy the Music.

'I was hard put to it to make the money. I was able to knock a good profit out of the land and the beasts and the men that worked for me; and then, when I came to turn the profit into solid pieces, I found that there was a world outside of my world, and it was truly bent on robbing me, and, what's more, it had thought hard for generations about the best way of doing it. It had made its scheme so carefully that I was as helpless among them people as the labourers were with me. Oh! they got me, and they squeezed me, and they marched off smiling with the heaviest part of my gain, and they told me to be a bit more polite or they'd break me into bits, and I was polite too. Ah! there's a big world outside the little world, and maybe there's a bigger world outside that, and grindstones in it for all the people that are squeezers in their own place.

'The price I thought fair for the crop was never the price I got from the jobbers. If I sold a cow or a horse I never got as much as half of what I reckoned on. There were rings and cliques in the markets everywhere, and they knew how to manage me. It was they who got more than half the money I made, and they had me gripped so that I couldn't get away.

It was for these people I used to be out of bed at twelve o'clock at night and up again before the fowl were done snoring, and it was for them I tore the bowels out of my land, and hazed and bedevilled every man and woman and dog that came in sight of me, and when I thought of these market-men with their red jowls and their "take it or leave it" I used to get so full of rage that I could hardly breathe.

'I had to take it because I couldn't afford to leave it, and then I'd go home again trying to cut it finer, trying to skin an extra chance profit off the land and workers, and I do wonder now that the men didn't try to kill me or didn't commit suicide. Aye, I wonder that I didn't commit suicide myself by dint of the rage and greed and weariness that was my share of life day and night.

'I got the money anyhow, and, sure enough, the people must have thought I was the devil's self; but it was little I cared what they thought, for the pieces were beginning to mount up in the box, and one fine day the box got so full that not another penny-piece could have been squeezed sideways into it, so I had to make a new box, and it wasn't so long until I made a third box and a fourth one, and I could see the time coming when I would be able to stand in with the market-men, and get a good grip on whatever might be going.'

'How much did you rob in all?' said Patsy.

'I had all of two thousand pounds.'

'That's a lot of money, I'm thinking.'

'It is so, and it took a lot of getting, and there was twenty damns went into the box with every one of the yellow pieces.'

'A damn isn't worth a shilling,' said Patsy. 'You can have them from me at two for a ha'penny, and there's lots of people would give them to yourself for nothing, you rotten old robber of the world! And if I had the lump of twist back that I gave you a couple of minutes ago I'd put it in my pocket, so I would, and I'd sit on it.'

'Don't forget that you're talking about old things,' said Billy the Music.

'If I was one of your men,' shouted Patsy, 'you wouldn't have treated me that way.'

Billy the Music smiled happily at him.

'Wouldn't I?' said he, with his head on one side.

'You would not,' said Patsy, 'for I'd have broken your skull with a spade.'

'If you had been one of my men,' the other replied mildly, 'you'd have been as tame as a little kitten; you'd have crawled round me with your hat in your hand and your eyes turned up like a dying duck's, and you'd have said, "Yes, sir," and "No, sir," like the other men that I welted the stuffing out of with my two fists, and broke the spirits of with labour and hunger. Don't be talking now, for you're an ignorant man in these things, although you did manage to steal a clocking hen off me the day I was busy.'

'And a pair of good boots,' said Patsy triumphantly.

'Do you want to hear the rest of the story?'

'I do so,' said Patsy; 'and I take back what I said about the tobacco; here's another bit of it for your pipe.'

'Thank you kindly,' replied Billy.

He shook the ashes from his pipe, filled it, and continued his tale.

'On the head of all these things a wonderful thing happened to me.'

'That's the way to start,' said Patsy approvingly. 'You're a good story-teller, mister.'

'It isn't so much that,' replied Billy, 'but it's a good story and a wonderful story.'

'The potatoes are nearly done, Mary, a grah?'

'They'll be done in a short while.'

'Hold your story for a few minutes until we eat the potatoes and a few collops of the rabbits, for I tell you that I'm drooping with the hunger.'

107

'I didn't eat anything myself,' replied Billy, 'since the middle of yesterday, and the food there has a smell to it that's making me mad.'

'It's not quite done yet,' said Mary.

'It's done enough,' replied her father. 'Aren't you particular this day! Pull them over here and share them round, and don't be having the men dying on your hands.'

Mary did so, and for five minutes there was no sound except that of moving jaws, and by that time there was no more food in sight.

'Ah!' said Patsy, with a great sigh.

'Aye, indeed!' said Billy the Music, with another sigh.

'Put on more of the potatoes now,' Patsy commanded his daughter, 'and be cooking them against the time this story will be finished.'

'I wish I had twice as much as I had,' said Art.

'You got twice as much as me,' cried Patsy angrily, 'for I saw the girl giving it to you.'

'I'm not complaining,' replied Art; 'I'm only stating a fact.'

'That's all right,' said Patsy.

The pipes were lit, and all eyes turned to Billy the Music. Patsy leaned back on his elbow, and blew his cloud.

'Now we'll have the rest of the story,' said he.

CHAPTER XXII

'THIS,' continued Billy the Music, 'is the wonderful thing that happened to me.

'Bit by bit I got fonder of the money. The more I got of it, the more I wanted. I used to go away by myself and look at it and handle it and count it. I didn't store it all in the house; I only kept enough there to make the people think it was all there, and as every one was watching that and watching each other (for they all wanted to steal it) it was safe enough.

'They didn't know it was mostly copper was in that box, but copper it was, and some silver that I couldn't fit into the other boxes.

'There was a place at the end of the big barn, just underneath the dog's kennel—maybe you remember my dog, Patsy?'

'A bit black-and-white snarly devil of a bull-terrier?' said Patsy thoughtfully.

'That's him.'

'I remember him well,' said Patsy. 'I fed him once.'

'You poisoned him,' said Billy the Music quickly.

'That's a hard word to say,' replied Patsy, scraping at his chin.

Billy the Music looked very fixedly at him, and he also scraped meditatively at his bristles.

'It doesn't matter now,' said he. 'That was the dog. I made a place under his kennel. It was well made. If you had pulled the kennel aside you'd have seen nothing but the floor. Down there I kept the three boxes of gold, and while I'd be looking at them the dog would be lurching around wondering why he wasn't allowed to eat people—I was a bit timid

109

with that dog myself—and it was one day while I was handling the money that the thing happened.

'There came a thump on the barn door. The dog made a noise away down in the heel of his throat and loped across; he stuck his nose against the crack at the bottom and began to sniff and scratch.

' "Strangers there," said I. I put the money away quietly, lifted the kennel back to its place, and went over to open the door.

'There were two men standing outside, and the dog sprang for one of them as if he had been shot out of a gun.

'But that man was quick. He took the beast on the jump, caught him by the chaps, and slung him with a heave of his arm. I don't know where he slung him to; I never saw the dog alive after that, and I did think it was that jerk killed him.'

'Begor!' said Patsy.

'It must have been within half an hour or so that you gave him the poisoned meat, Patsy.'

'It was a lengthy mutton bone,' murmured Mac Cann.

'Whatever it was!' said Billy the Music.

'The men walked in, they shut the barn door behind behind them and locked it, for the key was inside whenever I was.

'Well! I always had the use of my hands and my feet and my teeth, but I had no chance there, so in a few minutes I sat down on the kennel to get my breath back and to mop up the blood that was teeming out of my nose. The two men, I will say, were very quiet with it all—they waited for me.

'One of them was a middle-sized block of a man, and he looked as if his head had been rolled in tar——'

'Eh!' said Patsy loudly.

'The other one was a big, young man with a girl's face; he had blue eyes and curls of gold, and he was wearing a woman's skirt—the raggedest old——'

110

'Begor!' cried Patsy, and he leaped furiously to his feet.

'What's wrong with you?' said Billy the Music.

Patsy beat his fists together.

'I've been looking for that pair of playboys for a full year,' he barked.

'Do you know them?' said Billy the Music, with equal excitement.

'I don't know them, but I met them, and the girl yonder met them too, the thieves!'

'They are a pair of dirty dogs,' said Mary coldly.

'And when I do meet them,' said Patsy savagely, 'I'll kill the pair of them: I will so.'

Billy the Music laughed.

'I wouldn't try killing them lads; I did try it once, but they wouldn't let me. Tell us what they did to yourself, and then I'll go on with my story, for I'm real curious about those two.'

Mac Cann put his pipe into his pocket.

CHAPTER XXIII

SAID Patsy:

'There isn't very much to tell, but this is how it happened.

'About two weeks before your dog died, myself and the girl were tramping up towards Dublin. We hadn't got the ass with us that time, for it was in pawn to a woman that peddled fish in the south-west of Connemara. She was keeping the ass and cart for us while we were away, and she was going to give us something for their loan at the heel of the season. She was an old rip, that one, for she sold the ass on us to one man and she sold the cart to another man, and we had the trouble of the world getting the pair of them together again—but that's no matter.

'One morning, fresh and early, we were beating along a road that comes down from the mountains and runs away into Donnybrook. I had just picked up a little goose that I found walking along with its nose up, and I thought maybe we could sell the creature to some person in the city who wanted a goose.

'We turned a bend in the road (it's a twisty district), and there I saw two men sitting on the grass on each side of the path. The two men were sitting with the full width of the road between them, and they were clean, stark, stone naked.

'They hadn't got as much as a shirt; they hadn't a hat; they hadn't got anything at all on them barring their skins.

' "Whoo!" said I to myself, and I caught a grip of the girl. "We'll be taking another road," said I, and round we sailed with the goose and all.

'But the two men came after us, and what with the goose and the girl, they caught up on us too.

'One of them was a bullet-headed thief and he did look as if he had been rolled in tar, and I hope he was. The other was a dandy lad that never got his hair cut since he was a mother's boy.

' "Be off with the pair of you," said I, "ye indecent devils. What do ye want with honest folk and you in your pelt?"

'The bullet-headed one was bouncing round me like a rubber ball.

' "Take off your clothes, mister," said he.

' "What!" said I.

' "Take off your clothes quick," said he, "or I'll kill you."

'So, with that I jumped into the middle of the road, and I up with the goose, and I hit that chap such a welt on the head that the goose bursted. Then the lad was into me and we went round the road like thunder and lightning till the other fellow joined in, and then Mary welted into the lot of us with a stick that she had, but they didn't mind her any more than a fly. Before you could whistle, mister, they had me stripped to the buff, and before you could whistle again they had the girl stripped, and the pair of them were going down the road as hard as ever they could pelt with our clothes under their oxters.'

'Begor!' said Billy the Music.

'I tell you so,' grinned Patsy.

'There was herself and myself standing in the middle of the road with nothing to cover our nakedness but a bursted goose.'

'That was the queer sight,' said Billy the Music, looking thoughtfully at Mary.

'You keep your eyes to yourself, mister,' said Mary hotly.

'What did you do then?' said Billy.

'We sat down on the side of the road for a long time until we heard footsteps and then we hid ourselves.

'I peeped over the hedge, and there was a man coming along the path. He was a nice-looking man with a black bag

113

in his hand and he was walking fast. When he came exactly opposite me I jumped the hedge, and I took the clothes off him——'

Billy the Music slapped his palm on his knee.

'You did so!'

'I did so,' said Patsy.

'He was grumbling all the time, but as soon as I let him loose he started to run, and that was the last I saw of him.

'After a bit a woman came along the road, and Mary took the clothes off her. She was a quiet, poor soul, and she didn't say a word to either of us. We left her the goose and the man's black bag for payment, and then the pair of us started off, and we didn't stop running till we came to the County Kerry.

'These are the clothes I'm telling you about,' said Patsy; 'I have them on me this minute.'

'It's a great story,' said Billy the Music.

'I can tell you something further about these people,' said Caeltia, smiling.

'Can you so?' cried Patsy.

'I can, but the man here hasn't finished what he was telling us.'

'I was forgetting him,' said Mac Cann. 'Put another pinch in your pipe, mister, and tell us what happened to you after that.'

CHAPTER XXIV

BILLY THE MUSIC did put another pinch of tobacco into his pipe, and after drawing on it meditatively for a few minutes he snuffed it out with his thumb and put it into his pocket. Naturally he put it in upside down, so that the tobacco might drop from the pipe, for he was no longer a saving man.

'They were surely the two men that I'm telling you about,' said he; 'and there they were standing up in front of me while I was sneezing the blood out of my nose.

' "What do you want?" said I to themselves, and all the time I was peeping here and there to see if there wasn't a bit of a stick or a crowbar maybe lying handy.

'It was the boyo in the skirt that answered me:

' "I wanted to have a look at yourself," said he.

' "Take your eye-full and go away for God's sake," said I.

' "You dirty thief!" said he to me.

' "What's that for?" said I.

' "What do you mean by getting me thrown out of heaven?" said he.

'. . .! Well, mister honey, that was a question to worry any man, and it worried me. I couldn't think what to say to him. "Begor!" said I, and I sneezed out some more of my blood.

'But the lad was stamping mad.

' "If I could blot you from the light of life without doing any hurt to myself, I'd smash you this mortal minute," said he.

' "For the love of heaven," said I, "tell me what I did to yourself, for I never did see you before this day, and I wish I didn't see you now."

'The bullet-headed man was standing by all the time, and he chewing tobacco.

' "Have it out with him, Cuchulain," said he. "Kill him," said he, "and send him out among the spooks."

'But the other man calmed down a bit, and he came over to me wagging the girl's skirts.

' "Listen!" said he, "I'm the Seraph Cuchulain."

' "Very good," said I.

' "I'm your Guardian Angel," said he.

' "Very good," said I.

' "I'm your Higher Self," said he, "and every rotten business you do down here does be vibrating against me up there. You never did anything in your life that wasn't rotten. You're a miser and a thief, and you got me thrown out of heaven because of the way you loved money. You seduced me when I wasn't looking. You made a thief of me in a place where it's no fun to be a robber, and here I am wandering the dirty world on the head of your unrighteous ways. Repent, you beast," said he, and he landed me a clout on the side of the head that rolled me from one end of the barn to the other.

' "Give him another one," said the bullet-headed man, and he chewing strongly on his plug.

' "What have you got to do with it?" said I to him. "You're not my Guardian Angel, God help me!"

' "How dare you!" said the bullet-headed man. "How dare you set this honest party stealing the last threepenny-bit of a poor man?" and with that he made a clout at me.

' "What threepenny-bit are you talking about?" said I.

' "My own threepenny-bit," said he. "The only one I had. The one I dropped outside the gates of hell."

'Well, that beat me! "I don't care what you say any longer," said I, "you can talk till you're blue and I won't care what you say," and down I sat on the kennel and shed my blood.

' "You must repent of your own free will," said Cuchulain, marching to the door.

' "And you'd better hurry up, too," said the other fellow, "or I'll hammer the head off you."

'The queer thing is that I believed every word the man said. I didn't know what he was talking about, but I did know that he was talking about something that was real although it was beyond me. And there was the way he said it too, for he spoke like a bishop, with fine, shouting words that I can't remember now, and the months gone past. I took him at his word anyhow, and on the minute I began to feel a different creature, for, mind you, a man can no more go against his Guardian Angel than he can climb a tree backwards.

'As they were going out of the barn Cuchulain turned to me:

' "I'll help you to repent," said he, "for I want to get back again, and this is the way I'll help you. I'll give you money, and I'll give you piles of it."

'The two of them went off then, and I didn't venture out of the barn for half an hour.

'I went into the barn next day, and what do you think I saw?'

'The floor was covered with gold pieces,' said Patsy.

Billy nodded:

'That's what I saw. I gathered them up and hid them under the kennel. There wasn't room for the lot of them, so I rolled the rest in a bit of a sack and covered them up with cabbages.

'The next day I went in and the floor was covered with gold pieces, and I swept them up and hid them under the cabbages too. The day after that, and the next day, and the day after that again it was the same story. I didn't know where to put the money. I had to leave it lying on the floor, and I hadn't as much as a dog to guard it from the robbers.'

'You had not,' said Patsy, 'and that's the truth.'

'I locked the barn; then I called up all the men; I paid them their wages, for what did I want with them any longer and I rolling in gold? I told them to get out of my sight, and I saw every man of them off the land. Then I told my wife's brother that I didn't want him in my house any longer, and I saw him off the land. Then I argued my son out of the house, and I told my wife that she could go with him if she wanted to, and then I went back to the barn.

'But, as I told you a minute ago, I was a changed man. The gold was mounting up on me, and I didn't know what to do with it. I could have rolled in it if I wanted to, and I did roll in it, but there was no fun in that.

'This was the trouble with me—I couldn't count it; it had gone beyond me; there were piles of it; there were stacks of it; it was four feet deep all over the floor, and I could no more move it than I could move a house.

'I never wanted that much money, for no man could want it: I only wanted what I could manage with my hands; and the fear of robbers was on me to that pitch that I could neither sit nor stand nor sleep.

'Every time I opened the door the place was fuller than it was the last time, and, at last, I got to hate the barn. I just couldn't stand the look of the place, and the light squinting at me from thousands and thousands of gold corners.

'It beat me at last. One day I marched into the house, and I picked up the concertina that my son bought (I was able to play it well myself), and said I to the wife:

' "I'm off."

' "Where are you off?"

' "I'm going into the world."

' "What will become of the farm?"

' "You can have it yourself," said I, and with that I step-ped clean out of the house and away to the road. I didn't stop walking for two days, and I never went back from that day to this.

'I do play on the concertina before the houses, and the people give me coppers. I travel from place to place every day, and I'm as happy as a bird on a bough, for I've no worries and I worry no one.'

'What did become of the money?' said Patsy.

'I'm thinking now that it might have been fairy gold, and, if it was, nobody could touch it.'

'So,' said Mac Cann, 'that's the sort of boys they were?'

'That's the sort.'

'And one of them was your own Guardian Angel!'

'He said that.'

'And what was the other one?'

'I don't know, but I do think that he was a spook.'

Patsy turned to Finaun:

'Tell me, mister, is that a true story now, or was the lad making it up?'

'It is true,' replied Finaun.

Patsy considered for a moment.

'I wonder,' said he musingly, 'who is my own Guardian Angel?'

Caeltia hastily put the pipe into his pocket.

'I am,' said he.

'Oh, bedad!'

Mac Cann placed his hands on his knees and laughed heartily.

'You are! and I making you drunk every second night in the little pubs!'

'You never made me drunk.'

'I did not, for you've got a hard head surely, but there's a pair of us in it, mister.'

He was silent again, then:

'I wonder who is the Guardian Angel of Eileen Ni Cooley? for he has his work cut out for him, I'm thinking.'

'I am her Guardian Angel,' said Finaun.

'Are you telling me that?'

Mac Cann stared at Finaun, and he lapsed again to reverie.

'Ah, well!' said he to Billy the Music, 'it was a fine story you told us, mister, and queer deeds you were mixed up in; but I'd like to meet the men that took our clothes, I would so.'

'I can tell you something more about them,' Caeltia remarked.

'So you said a while back. What is it you can tell us?'

'I can tell you the beginning of all that tale.'

'I'd like to hear it,' said Billy the Music.

'There is just a piece I will have to make up from what I heard since we came here, but the rest I can answer for because I was there at the time.'

'I remember it too,' said Art to Caeltia, 'and when you have told your story I'll tell another one.'

'Serve out the potatoes, Mary,' said Mac Cann, 'and then you can go on with the story. Do you think is that ass all right, alannah?'

'He's eating the grass still, but I think he may be wanting a drink.'

'He had a good drink yesterday,' said her father, and he shifted to a more comfortable position.

CHAPTER XXV

SAID Caeltia:

'When Brien O'Brien died, people said that it did not matter very much because he would have died young in any case. He would have been hanged, or his head would have been split in two halves with a hatchet, or he would have tumbled down the cliff when he was drunk and been smashed into jelly. Something like that was due to him, and everybody likes to see a man get what he deserves to get.

'But, as ethical writs cease to run when a man is dead, the neighbours did not stay away from his wake. They came and they said many mitigating things across the body with the bandaged jaws and the sly grin, and they reminded each other of this and that queer thing which he had done, for his memory was crusted over with stories of wild, laughable things, and other things which were wild but not laughable.

'Meanwhile he was dead, and one was at liberty to be a trifle sorry for him. Further, he belonged to the O'Brien nation—a stock to whom reverence was due. A stock not easily forgotten. The historic memory could reconstruct forgotten glories of station and battle, of terrible villainy and terrible saintliness, the pitiful, valorous, slow descent to the degradation which was not yet wholly victorious. A great stock! The O'Neills remembered it. The O'Tools and the Mac Sweeneys had stories by the hundred of love and hate. The Burkes and the Geraldines and the new strangers had memories also.

'His family was left in the poorest way, but they were used to that, for he had kept them as poor as he left them, or found them, for that matter. They had shaken hands with

121

Charity so often that they no longer disliked the sallow-faced lady, and so certain small gifts made by the neighbours were accepted, not very thankfully, but very readily. These gifts were almost always in kind. A few eggs. A bag of potatoes. A handful of meal. A couple of twists of tea—such like.

'One of the visitors, however, moved by an extraordinary dejection, slipped a silver threepenny-piece into the hand of Brien's little daughter, Sheila, aged four years, and later on she did not like to ask for it back again.

'Little Sheila had been well trained by her father. She knew exactly what should be done with money, and so, when nobody was looking, she tiptoed to the coffin and slipped the threepenny-piece into Brien's hand. That hand had never refused money when it was alive, it did not reject it either when it was dead.

'They buried him the next day.

'He was called up for judgment the day after, and made his appearance with a miscellaneous crowd of wretches, and there he again received what was due to him. He was removed protesting and struggling to the place decreed:

'"Down," said Rhadamanthus, pointing with his great hand, and down he went.

'In the struggle he dropped the threepenny-piece, but he was so bustled and heated that he did not observe his loss. He went down, far down, out of sight, out of remembrance, to a howling black gulf with others of his unseen kind.

'A young seraph, named Cuchulain, chancing to pass that way shortly afterwards, saw the threepenny-piece peeping brightly from the rocks, and he picked it up.

'He looked at it in astonishment. He turned it over and over, this way and that way. Examined it at the stretch of his arm, and peered minutely at it from two inches distance.

'"I have never in my life seen anything so beautifully wrought," said he, and, having stowed it in his pouch along

122

with some other trinkets, he strolled homewards again through the massy gates.

'It was not long until Brien discovered his loss, and suddenly, through the black region, his voice went mounting and brawling.

' "I have been robbed," he yelled. "I have been robbed in heaven!"

'Having begun to yell he did not stop. Sometimes he was simply angry and made a noise. Sometimes he became sarcastic and would send his query swirling upwards.

' "Who stole the threepenny-bit?" he roared. He addressed the surrounding black space:

' "Who stole the last threepenny-bit of a poor man?"

'Again and again his voice pealed upwards. The pains of his habitation lost all their sting for him. His mind had nourishment, and the heat within him vanquished the fumes without. He had a grievance, a righteous cause, he was buoyed and strengthened, nothing could silence him. They tried ingenious devices, all kinds of complicated things, but he paid no heed, and the tormentors were in despair.

' "I hate these sinners from the kingdom of Kerry," said the Chief Tormentor, and he sat moodily down on his own circular saw; and that worried him also, for he was clad only in a loin-cloth.

' "I hate the entire Clann of the Gael," said he; "why cannot they send them somewhere else?" and then he started practising again on Brien.

'It was no use. Brien's query still blared upwards like the sound of the great trump itself. It wakened and rung the rocky caverns, screamed through fissure and funnel, and was battered and slung from pinnacle to crag and up again. Worse! his companions in doom became interested and took up the cry, until at last the uproar became so appalling that the Master himself could not stand it.

' "I have not had a wink of sleep for three nights," said

123

that harassed one, and he sent a special embassy to the powers.

'Rhadamanthus was astonished when they arrived. His elbow was leaning on his vast knee, and his heavy head rested on a hand that was acres long, acres wide.

' "What is all this about?" said he.

' "The Master cannot go to sleep," said the spokesman of the embassy, and he grinned as he said it, for it sounded queer even to himself.

' "It is not necessary that he should sleep," said Rhadamanthus. "I have never slept since time began, and I will never sleep until time is over. But the complaint is curious. What has troubled your master?"

' "Hell is turned upside down and inside out," said the fiend. "The tormentors are weeping like little children. The principalities are squatting on their hunkers doing nothing. The orders are running here and there fighting each other. The styles are leaning against walls shrugging their shoulders, and the damned are shouting and laughing and have become callous to torment."

' "It is not my business," said the judge.

' "The sinners demand justice," said the spokesman.

' "They've got it," said Rhadamanthus, "let them stew in it."

' "They refuse to stew," replied the spokesman, wringing his hands.

'Rhadamanthus sat up.

' "It is an axiom in law," said he, "that however complicated an event may be, there can never be more than one person at the extreme bottom of it. Who is the person?"

' "It is one Brien of the O'Brien nation, late of the kingdom of Kerry. A bad one! He got the maximum punishment a week ago."

'For the first time in his life Rhadamanthus was disturbed.

124

He scratched his head, and it was the first time he had ever done that either.

' "You say he got the maximum," said Rhadamanthus, "then it's a fix! I have damned him for ever, and better or worse than that cannot be done. It is none of my business," said he angrily, and he had the deputation removed by force.

'But that did not ease the trouble. The contagion spread until ten million billions of voices were chanting in unison, and uncountable multitudes were listening between their pangs.

' "Who stole the threepenny-bit? Who stole the threepenny-bit?"

'That was still their cry. Heaven rang with it as well as hell. Space was filled with that rhythmic tumult. Chaos and empty Nox had a new discord added to their elemental throes. Another memorial was drafted below, showing that unless the missing coin was restored to its owner hell would have to close its doors. There was a veiled menace in the memorial also, for Clause 6 hinted that if hell was allowed to go by the board heaven might find itself in some jeopardy thereafter.

'The document was despatched and considered. In consequence a proclamation was sent through all the wards of Paradise, calling on whatever person, archangel, seraph, cherub, or acolyte, had found a threepenny-piece since midday of the 10th August then instant, that the same person, archangel, seraph, cherub, or acolyte, should deliver the said threepenny-piece to Rhadamanthus at his Court, and should receive in return a free pardon and a receipt.

'The coin was not delivered.

'The young seraph, Cuchulain, walked about like a person who was strange to himself. He was not tormented: he was angry. He frowned, he cogitated and fumed. He drew one golden curl through his fingers until it was lank and

125

drooping; save the end only, that was still a ripple of gold. He put the end in his mouth and strode moodily chewing it. And every day his feet turned in the same direction—down the long entrance boulevard, through the mighty gates, along the strip of carved slabs, to that piled wilderness where Rhadamanthus sat monumentally.

'Here delicately he went, sometimes with a hand outstretched to help his foothold, standing for a space to think ere he jumped to a farther rock, balancing himself for a moment ere he leaped again. So he would come to stand and stare gloomily upon the judge.

'He would salute gravely, as was meet, and say, "God bless the work"; but Rhadamanthus never replied, save by a nod, for he was very busy.

'Yet the judge did observe him, and would sometimes heave ponderous lids to where he stood, and so, for a few seconds, they regarded each other in an interval of that unceasing business.

'Sometimes for a minute or two the young seraph Cuchulain would look from the judge to the judged as they crouched back or strained forward, the good and the bad all in the same tremble of fear, all unknowing which way their doom might lead. They did not look at each other. They looked at the judge high on his ebon throne, and they could not look away from him. There were those who knew, guessed clearly their doom; abashed and flaccid they sat, quaking. There were some who were uncertain—rabbit-eyed these, not less quaking than the others, biting at their knuckles as they peeped upwards. There were those hopeful, yet searching fearfully backwards in the wilderness of memory, chasing and weighing their sins; and these last, even when their bliss was sealed and their steps set on an easy path, went faltering, not daring to look around again, their ears strained to catch a—"Halt, miscreant! this other is your way!"

'So, day by day, he went to stand near the judge; and one day Rhadamanthus, looking on him more intently, lifted his great hand and pointed:

'"Go you among those to be judged," said he.

'For Rhadamanthus knew. It was his business to look deep into the heart and the mind, to fish for secrets in the pools of being.

'And the young seraph Cuchulain, still rolling his golden curl between his lips, went obediently forward and set down his nodding plumes between two who whimpered and stared and quaked.

'When his turn came, Rhadamanthus eyed him intently for a long time:

'"Well!" said Rhadamanthus.

'The young seraph Cuchulain blew the curl of gold from his lips:

'"Findings are keepings," said he loudly, and he closed his mouth and stared very impertinently at the judge.

'"It is to be given up," said the judge.

'"Let them come and take it from me," said the seraph Cuchulain. And suddenly (for these things are at the will of spirits) around his head the lightnings span, and his hands were on the necks of thunders.

'For the second time in his life Rhadamanthus was disturbed, again he scratched his head:

'"It's a fix," said he moodily. But in a moment he called to those whose duty it was:

'"Take him to this side," he roared.

'And they advanced. but the seraph Cuchulain swung to meet them, and his golden hair blazed and shrieked; and the thunders rolled at his feet, and about him a bright network that hissed and stung—and those who advanced turned haltingly backwards and ran screaming.

'"It's a fix," said Rhadamanthus; and for a little time he stared menacingly at the seraph Cuchulain.

'But only for a little time. Suddenly he put his hands on the rests of his throne and heaved upwards his terrific bulk. Never before had Rhadamanthus stood from his ordained chair. He strode mightily forward and in an instant had quelled that rebel. The thunders and lightnings were but moonbeams and dew on that stony carcass. He seized the seraph Cuchulain, lifted him to his breast as one lifts a sparrow, and tramped back with him:

'"Fetch me that other," said he sternly, and he sat down.

'Those whose duty it was sped swiftly downwards to find Brien of the O'Brien nation; and while they were gone, all in vain the seraph Cuchulain crushed flamy barbs against that bosom of doom. Now, indeed, his golden locks were drooping and his plumes were broken and tossed; but his fierce eye still glared courageously against the nipple of Rhadamanthus.

'Soon they brought Brien. He was a sight of woe— howling, naked as a tree in winter, black as a tarred wall, carved and gashed, tattered in all but his throat, wherewith, until one's ears rebelled, he bawled his one demand.

'But the sudden light struck him to a wondering silence, and the sight of the judge holding the seraph Cuchulain like a limp flower to his breast held him gaping.

'"Bring him here," said Rhadamanthus.

'And they brought him to the steps of the throne.

'"You have lost a medal!" said Rhadamanthus. "This one has it."

'Brien looked straitly at the seraph Cuchulain.

'Rhadamanthus stood again, whirled his arm in an enormous arc, jerked, and let go, and the seraph Cuchulain went swirling through space like a slung stone.

'"Go after him, Kerryman," said Rhadamanthus, stooping; and he seized Brien by the leg, whirled him wide and out and far; dizzy, dizzy as a swooping comet, and down, and down, and down.

'Rhadamanthus seated himself. He motioned with his hand.

' "Next," said he coldly.

'Down went the seraph Cuchulain, swirling in wide tumbles, scarcely visible for quickness. Sometimes, with outstretched hands, he was a cross that dropped plumb. Anon, head urgently downwards, he dived steeply. Again, like a living hoop, head and heels together, he spun giddily. Blind, deaf, dumb, breathless, mindless; and behind him Brien of the O'Brien nation came pelting and whizzing.

'What of that journey? Who could give it words? Of the suns that appeared and disappeared like winkling eyes. Comets that shone for an instant, went black and vanished. Moons that came, and stood, and were gone. And around all, including all, boundless space, boundless silence; the black unmoving void—the deep, unending quietude, through which they fell with Saturn and Orion, and mildly-smiling Venus, and the fair, stark-naked moon, and the decent earth wreathed in pearl and blue. From afar she appeared, the quiet one, all lonely in the void. As sudden as a fair face in a crowded street. Beautiful as the sound of falling waters. Beautiful as the sound of music in a silence. Like a white sail on a windy sea. Like a green tree in a solitary place. Chaste and wonderful she appeared. Flying afar. Flying aloft like a joyous bird when the morning breaks on the darkness and he shrills sweet tidings. She soared and sang. Gently she sang to timid pipes and flutes of tender straw and murmuring, distant strings. A song that grew and swelled, gathering to a multitudinous, deep-thundered harmony, until the overburdened ear failed before the appalling uproar of her ecstasy, and denounced her. No longer a star! No longer a bird! A plumed and horned fury! Gigantic, gigantic, leaping and shrieking tempestuously, spouting whirlwinds of lightning, tearing gluttonously along her path, avid, rampant, howling with rage and terror she leaped, dreadfully she leaped and flew. . . .

'Enough! They hit the earth—they were not smashed, there was that virtue in them. They hit the ground just outside the village of Donnybrook where the back road runs to the hills; and scarcely had they bumped twice when Brien of the O'Brien nation had the seraph Cuchulain by the throat.

' "My threepenny-bit," he roared, with one fist up.

'But the seraph Cuchulain only laughed:

' "That!" said he. "Look at me, man. Your little medal dropped far beyond the rings of Saturn."

'And Brien stood back looking at him—He was as naked as Brien was. He was as naked as a stone, or an eel, or a pot, or a new-born babe. He was very naked.

'So Brien of the O'Brien nation strode across the path and sat down by the side of a hedge:

' "The first man that passes this way," said he, "will give me his clothes, or I'll strangle him."

'The seraph Cuchulain walked over to him:

' "I will take the clothes of the second man that passes," said he, and he sat down.'

CHAPTER XXVI

'AND then,' said Mac Cann thoughtfully, 'we came along, and they stole our clothes.'

'That wasn't a bad tale,' he continued to Caeltia. 'You are as good a story-teller, mister, as the man himself,' pointing to Billy the Music.

Billy replied modestly:

'It's because the stories were good ones that they were well told, for that's not my trade, and what wonder would it be if I made a botch of it? I'm a musician myself, as I told you, and there's my instrument, but I knew an old man in Connaught one time, and he was a great lad for the stories. He used to make his money at it, and if that man was to break off in the middle of a tale the people would stand up and kill him, they would so. He was a gifted man, for he would tell you a story about nothing at all, and you'd listen to him with your mouth open and you afraid that he would come to the end of it soon, and maybe it would be nothing more than the tale of how a white hen laid a brown egg. He would tell you a thing you knew all your life, and you would think it was a new thing. There was no old age in that man's mind, and that's the secret of story-telling.'

Said Mary:

'I could listen to a story for a day and a night.'

Her father nodded acquiescence:

'So could I, if it was a good story and well told, and I would be ready to listen to another one after that.'

He turned to Art:

'You were saying yourself, sonny, that there was a story in your head, and if that's so now is your chance to tell it; but

'I'm doubting you'll be able to do it as well as the two men here, for you are a youngster, and story-telling is an old man's trade.'

'I'll do my best,' said Art, 'but I never told a story in my life, and it may not be a good one at the first attempt.'

'That's all right,' replied Mac Cann encouragingly. 'We won't be hard on you.'

'Sure enough,' said Billy the Music, 'and you've listened to the lot of us, so you will know the road.'

'What are you going to talk about?' said Caeltia.

'I'm going to talk about Brien O'Brien, the same as the rest of you.'

'Did you know him too?' cried Billy.

'I did.'

'There isn't a person doesn't know that man,' growled Patsy. 'Maybe'—and he grinned ferociously as he said it—'maybe we'll meet him on the road and he tramping, and perhaps he will tell us a story himself.'

'That man could not tell a story,' Finaun interrupted, 'for he has no memory, and that is a thing a good story-teller ought to have.'

'If we meet him,' said Mac Cann grimly, 'I'll do something to him and he'll remember it, and it's likely that he will be able to make a story out of it too.'

'I only saw him once,' said Art, 'but when Rhadamanthus tossed him through the void I recognised his face, although so long a time had elapsed since I did see him. He is now less than he was, but he is, nevertheless, much more than I had expected he would be.'

'What is he now?' said Billy the Music.

'He is a man.'

'We are all that,' said Patsy, 'and it isn't any trouble to us.'

'It was more trouble than you imagine,' said Finaun.

'I had expected him to be no more than one of the higher

132

animals, or even that he might have been dissipated completely from existence.'

'What was he at the time you met him?'

'He was a magician, and he was one of the most powerful magicians that ever lived. He was a being of the fifth round, and he had discovered many secrets.'

'I have known magicians,' commented Finaun, 'and I always found that they were fools.'

'Brien O'Brien destroyed himself,' Art continued, 'he forfeited his evolution and added treble to his karmic burden because he had not got a sense of humour.'

'No magician has a sense of humour,' remarked Finaun, 'he could not be a magician if he had—Humour is the health of the mind.'

'That,' Art broke in, 'is one of the things he said to me. So you see he had discovered something. He was very near to being a wise man. He was certainly a courageous man, or, perhaps, foolhardy; but he was as serious as a fog, and he could not bring himself to believe it.'

'Tell us the story,' said Caeltia.

'Here it is,' said Art.

CHAPTER XXVII

'ON a day long ago I laboured with the Army of the Voice. The first syllable of the great word had been uttered, and in far eastern space, beyond seven of the flaming wheels, I and the six sons drew the lives together and held them for the whirlwind which is the one. We were waiting for the second syllable to form the wind.

'As I stood by my place holding the north in quietness, I felt a strong vibration between my hands. Something was interfering with me. I could not let go, but I looked behind, and there I saw a man standing, and he was weaving spells.

'It was a short, dark man with a little bristle of black whisker on his chin and a stiff bristle of black hair on his head. He was standing inside a double triangle having the points upwards, and there were magical signs at each point of the triangles. While I looked, he threw around him from side to side a flaming circle, and then he threw a flaming circle about him from front to back, and he span these so quickly that he was surrounded by a wall of fire.

'At him, on the instant, I charged a bolt, but it could not penetrate his cricles; it hit them and fell harmless, for the circles had a greater speed than my thunderbolt.

'He stood so in the triangles, laughing at me and scratching his chin.

'I dared not loose my hands again lest the labour of a cycle should be dissipated in an instant, and it was no use shouting to the others, for they also were holding the lives in readiness for the whirlwind which would shape them to a globe, so the man had me at his mercy.

'He was working against my grip, and he had amazing

power. He had somehow discovered part of the first syllable of the great word, and he was intoning this on me between giggles, but he could not destroy us, for together we were equal to the number of that syllable.

'When I looked at him again he laughed at me, and what he said astonished me greatly.

' "This," said he, "is very funny."

'I made no reply to him, being intent only on holding my grip; but I was reassured, for, although he poured on me incessantly the great sound, its effect was neutralised, for I am a number, and in totality we were the numbers; nevertheless the substance did strain and heave so powerfully that I could do no more than hold it in place.

'The man spoke to me again. Said he:

' "Do you not think that this is very funny?"

'I made no answer for a time, and then I said:

' "Who are you?"

' "A name," he replied, "is a power; I won't give you my name although I would like to, for this is a great deed and a funny one."

' "What is your planet?" quoth I.

' "I won't tell you that," he replied, "you might read my signs and come after me later on."

'I could not but admire the immense impertinence of his deed.

' "I know your sign," said I, "for you have already made it three times with your hand, and there is only one planet of these systems which has evolved the fifth race, so I know your planet. Your symbol is the Mule, and Uriel is your Regent; he will be coming after you soon, so you had better go away while you have time."

' "If he comes," said the man, "I'll put him in a bottle, and I'll put you in a bottle too. I won't go for another while, the joke is too good, and this is only the commencement of it."

' "You will be caught by the second syllable," I warned him.

' "I'll put it in a bottle," said he, grinning at me. "No," he continued, "I won't be caught, I've made my calculations, and it's not due yet a while."

'Again he poured on me the great sound until I rocked to and fro like a bush in the wind; but he could not loose my grip, for I was a part of the word.

' "Why are you doing this?" I asked him.

' "I'll tell you that," he replied.

' "I am two things, and I am great in each of these two things. I am a great magician, and I am a great humourist. Now, it is very easy to prove that one is a magician, for one has only to do things and then people are astonished; they are filled with fear and wonder; they fall down and worship and call one god and master. But it is not so easy to be a humourist, because in that case it is necessary to make people laugh. If a man is to be a magician it is necessary, if his art is to be appreciated, that the people around him be fools. If a person desires to be a humourist it is necessary that the people around him shall be at least as wise as he is, otherwise his humour will not be comprehended. You see my predicament! and it is a cruel one, for I cannot forego either of these ambitions—they are my karma. Laughter is purely an intellectual quality, and in my planet I have no intellectual equals: my jokes can only be enjoyed by myself, and it is of the essence of humour that one share it, or it turns to ill-health and cynicism and mental sourness. My humour cannot be shared with the people of my planet, for they are all half a round beneath me—they can never see the joke, they only see consequences, and these blind them to the rich drollery of any affair, and render me discontented and angry. My humour is too great for them, for it is not terrestrial but cosmic; it can only be appreciated by the gods, therefore I have come out here to seek my peers and to have at least one hearty laugh with them.

' "One must laugh," he continued, "for laughter is the

health of the mind, and I have not laughed for a crore of seasons."

'Thereupon he took up the syllable and intoned its flooding sound so that the matter beneath my hands strained against me almost unbearably.

'I turned my head and stared at the little man as he laughed happily to himself and scraped his chin.

' "You are a fool," said I to that man.

'The smile vanished from his face and a shade of dejection took its place.

' "Is it possible, Regent, that you have no sense of humour!" said he.

' "This," I replied, "is not humorous; it is only a practical joke; it is no more than incipient humour; there is no joke in it but only mischief, for to interfere with work is the humour of a babe or a monkey. You are a thoroughly serious person, and you will not make a joke in ten eternities; that also is in your karma."

'At these words his eyes brooded on me darkly, and an expression of real malignancy came on his face: he stamped at me from the triangles and hissed with rage.

' "I'll show you something else," said he, "and if it doesn't make you laugh it will make everybody else who hears about it laugh for an age."

'I saw that he was meditating a personal evil to me, but I was powerless, for I could not let go my grip on the substance.

'He lifted his hands against me then, but, at the moment, there came a sound, so low, so deep, it could scarcely be heard, and with equal strong intensity the sound pervaded all the spaces and brooded in every point and atom with its thrilling breath—we were about to shape to the whirlwind.

'The man's hands fell, and he stared at me.

' "Oh!" said he, and he said "Oh" three times in a whisper.

'The sound was the beginning of the second syllable.

'"I thought I had time," he gasped: "my calculations were wrong."

'"The joke is against you," said I to the man.

'"What will I do?" he screamed.

'"Laugh," I replied, "laugh at the joke."

'Already his flying circles had ceased to revolve, and their broad flame was no more than a blue flicker than disappeared even as I looked at them. He stood only in the triangles, and he was open to my vengeance. His staring, haggard eyes fell on the bolt in my hand.

'"There is no need for that," said he, and he did speak with some small dignity; "I am caught by the sound, and there is an end to me."

'And that was true, so I did not loose my bolt.

'Already his triangles were crumbling. He sank on his haunches, clasped his hands about his legs, and bowed his head on his knees. I could see that he knew all was lost, and that he was making a last desperate effort to guard his entity from dissolution, and he succeeded, for one instant before the triangles had disappeared he had vanished; but he could not have entirely escaped the sound, that was impossible, and if he reached his planet it must have been as a life of the third round instead of the fifth to which he had attained. He had the entire of his evolution to perform over again and had, moreover, added weightily to his karmic disabilities.

'I saw him no more, nor did I hear of him again until the day when Brien O'Brien was thrown from the gates, and then I knew that he and O'Brien were the same being, and that he had really escaped and was a fourth found life of the lowest globe.

'Perhaps he will be heard of again, for he is an energetic and restless being to whom an environment is an enemy and to whom humour is an ambition and a mystery.

'That is the end of my story,' said Art modestly.

Mac Cann regarded him indulgently from a cloud of smoke:

'It wasn't as good as the other ones,' he remarked, 'but that's not your fault, and you're young into the bargain.'

'He is not as young as he looks,' remarked Finaun.

'A good story has to be about ordinary things,' continued Patsy, 'but there isn't anybody could tell what your story was about.'

Billy the Music here broke in:

'The person I would have liked to hear more of is Cuchulain, for he is my own Guardian Angel and it's him I'm interested in. The next time I meet him I'll ask him questions.'

He glanced around the circle:

'Is there anybody would like to hear a tune on the concertina? I have it by my hand here, and the evening is before us.'

'You can play it for us the next time we meet,' said Patsy, 'for we are all tired listening to the stories, and you are tired yourself.'

He lifted to his feet then and yawned heartily with his arms at full stretch and his fists clenched:

'We had better be moving,' he continued, 'for the evening is coming on and it's twenty miles to the fair.'

They harnessed the ass.

'I'm going the opposite way to you,' said Billy the Music.

'All right,' said Patsy. 'God be with you, mister.'

'God be with yourselves,' replied Billy the Music.

He tramped off then in his own direction, while Mac Cann and his companions took their road with the ass.

BOOK IV

MARY MAC CANN

CHAPTER XXVIII

THE search for work and food led them back, but by different paths, through Kerry, up into Connemara, and thence by stony regions to Donegal again and the rugged hills.

Their days were uneventful but they were peaceful: their nights were pleasant, and seldom did they lack for even one meal in the day. When they did so lack they passed the unwelcome hour in the silence of those to whom such an hiatus was not singular. Under Mac Cann's captaincy the tiny band moved from meal to meal as another army would invest and sack and depart from the cities on its route.

Sometimes at night a ballad-singer would stray on their road, an angry man from whom no person had purchased songs for two days, and in return for victual this one would entertain them with his lays and recite the curses he had composed against those who did not pay the musician.

Sometimes they came on gatherings of tinkers and pedlars, tramps and trick-men, and in the midst of these they would journey towards a fair. Uproarious nights then! Wild throats yelling at the stars and much loud trampling on the roads as the women fought and screeched, and the men howled criticism and encouragement, and came by mere criticism themselves to the battle. Paltry onslaughts these, more of word than of weapon, to the fray that left some blooded noses and swollen lips as the one-hour memorial of their deeds.

And again the peaceful nights, the calm stars, the quiet moon strewing her path in silver; space for the eye, the ear, and the soul; the whispering of lovely trees; the unending rustle of the grass, and the wind that came and went away and came, chanting its long rhythms or hushing its chill lullaby by the fields and the hills.

On a day when they had finished eating, Finaun beckoned Caeltia and Art aside and they spoke closely together. Turning to Mac Cann and his daughter, Finaun said:

'We have finished what we came to do, my friends.'

Patsy nodded frowningly at him.

'What was it you came to do?'

'I came to give help to the powers,' said Finaun mildly.

'I didn't see you doing much,' replied Patsy.

'And,' Finaun continued smilingly, 'the time has come for us to go away.'

'You're in a hurry, I suppose?'

'We are not in a great hurry, but the time has come for us to go back.'

'Very well!' said Patsy. 'We aren't so far from where we started. If we take one of the turns on the right here, and bear away to the west by Cnuc-Mahon and Tober-Fola and Rath-Cormac, we'll come to the place where your things are buried, and then I suppose—we can get there in three days, if that will do you?'

'That will do,' said Finaun.

During the remainder of the day he and his companions walked together talking among themselves while Mac Cann and his daughter went with the ass.

Patsy also was preoccupied all that day, and she had her own thoughts; they scarcely spoke at all, and the ass was bored.

At night they camped under a broken arch, the vestige of they knew not what crumbled building, and, seated around the brazier, they sunk to silence, each staring at the red glow and thinking according to their need, and it was then that Art, lifting his eyes from the brazier, looked for the first time at Mary and saw that she was beautiful.

She had been looking at him—that was now her one

144

occupation. She existed only in these surreptitious examinations. She dwelt on him broodingly as a miser burns on his gold or a mother hovers hungrily upon her infant, but he had never given her any heed. Now he was looking at her, and across the brazier their eyes communed deeply.

There was birth already between them—sex was born, and something else was shaping feebly to existence. Love, that protection and cherishing, that total of life, the shy prince scarcely to be known among the teeming populations of the world, raised languidly from enchanted sleep a feeble hand.

What fire did their eyes utter! The quiet night became soundingly vocal. Winged words were around her again as in that twilight when her heart loosed its first trials of song. Though the night was about her black and calm there was dawn and sunlight in her heart, and she bathed herself deeply in the flame.

And he! There is no knowing but this, that his eyes poured soft fire, enveloping, exhaustless. He surrounded her as with a sea. There she slid and fell and disappeared, to find herself again, renewed, reborn, thrilling to the embrace of those waters, wondrously alive and yet so languid that she could not move. There she rocked like a boat on the broad waves and, saving the limitless sea, there was nothing in sight. Almost he even had disappeared from her view but not from her sensation: he was an influence wide as the world, deep and steep and tremendous as all space.

They were alone. The quiet men seated beside them thinned and faded and disappeared: the night whisked from knowledge as a mounting plume of smoke that eddies and is gone: the trees and the hills tripped softly backwards and drooped away. Now they were in a world of their own, microscopic, but intense: a sphere bounded by less than the stretching of their arms: a circle of such violent movement that it was stationary as a spinning-top, and her mind

145

whirled to it, and was still from very activity. She could not think, she could not try to think, that was her stillness, but she could feel and that was her movement; she was no longer a woman but a responsiveness: she was an universal contact thrilling at every pore and point: she was surrendered and lost and captured and no longer pertained to herself.

So much can the eye do when the gathered body peers meaningly through its lens. They existed in each other: in and through each other: the three feet of distance was no longer there: it had disappeared, and they were one being swinging on league-long wings through vast spaces.

When they dropped to sleep it was merely a slipping backwards, a motion that they did not feel: they were asleep before they dropped asleep: they were asleep long before that, drugged and senseless with the strong potion of the body, stronger than aught in the world but the sharp essence of the mind that awakens all things and never permits them to be lulled again.

When morning dawned and the camp awakened there was some little confusion, for Mac Cann was not in the place where he had slept and they could not imagine where he had gone to.

Mary discussed his disappearance in all kinds of terms, Caeltia alone, with a downcast air, refusing to speak of it. They waited during hours for him, but he did not return, and at noon they decided to wait no longer but to go on their journey, leaving him to catch on them if he was behind, or hoping to gain on him if he was in advance, for their route was marked.

The angels did seem a trifle lost in his absence, and they looked with some dubiety at Mary when she took charge of their journey and of the daily provision of their food.

Food had to be gotten, and she had to discover it not

alone for herself but for these other mouths. It was the first time she had been alone and, although her brows and lips were steady, her heart beat terror through her body.

For she had to do two things which she had never done and had never surmised really had to be done. She had to think, and she had to follow her thought by doing the thing she thought of. Which of these two was the more terrible she did not know, but there was no difficulty as to which she must do first, the simple orderliness of logic clamoured that she must think before she could do anything, and, so, her brain set to the painful weaving of webs too flimsy at first for any usage; but on this day she discovered where her head lay and how to use it without any assistance. She had memory to work with also, the recollection of her father's activities, and memory is knowledge; a well-packed head and energy— that is the baggage for life, it is the baggage for eternity.

She moved to the head of the ass and pulled his ear to advance. Caeltia and Finaun trod beside and they went forward. Behind came Art sniffing with the hungriest of nostrils on the sunny air, for it was five hours since they had eaten, and more than three hours' abstinence was painful to him.

CHAPTER XXIX

SHE did get food. She nourished her three children sumptuously, but she made them help her to get it.

She looked at Finaun's high nose, his sweeping beard, his air as of a good child well matured, and she sent it to the market:

'One must eat,' said she.

When they came to a house by the roadside she ordered Finaun to the door to ask for bread; he got it too, and had eaten but the slowest mouthful when she seized it from him and stocked it for the common good.

She charged Caeltia through the open door of a cottage, and his expedition was famous for eight hours afterwards.

She performed feats herself in a fowl-house and a cattle-pen, but she did not issue any commands to Art except at the falling-to, when he obeyed adequately.

She recalled the deeds of her father in many predicaments, and for the first time she really understood his ceaseless skill and activity. She found too that she could recollect his tactics, beside which her own were but childish blunderings, and, with that memory, she mended her hand, and life became the orderly progression which everybody expects it to be.

That night by the glow of the brazier she rested a mind that had never been weary before, and she craved for the presence of her father that she might gain from him the praise which her present companions did not know was due to her.

'Two days more,' said her heart, communicating to her

bitterly as they proceeded on the morrow morning, but she banished the thought and set to her plots and plans. She banished it, but it clung with her, vague and weighty as a nightmare, and when she looked backwards on the road Art's eyes were looking into hers with a quietness that almost drove her mad. She could not understand him.

They had never spoken to each other; not once had they spoken directly since that night when he stepped into the glow of a brazier. At first she had fled from him in a fear which was all shyness and wildness, and so an overlooking habit had been formed between them which he had never sought to break, and which she did not know how to put an end to.

'Two days!' said her heart again, pealing it to her through her webs, and again she exiled her heart, and could feel its wailing when she could hear it no longer.

They stopped for the midday meal; bread and potatoes and a morsel of cheese; the fare was plentiful, and from a stream near by good water washed it down.

The reins of the donkey were thrown across the limb of a tree, and he had liberty to browse in a circle. He also had his drink from the running stream, and was glad of it.

As they sat three people marched the road behind them; they saw these people, and studied their advance.

A talkative, a disorderly advance it was. An advance that halted every few paces for parley, and moved on again like a battle.

Two men and a woman were in that party, and it did seem that they were fighting every inch of their way. Certainly, they were laughing also for a harsh peal came creaking up the road, and came again. Once the laugh broke abruptly on its gruff note as though a hand had pounded into its middle. Then the party parleyed again and moved again.

What they said could not be distinguished, but the

rumour of their conversation might have been heard across the world. They bawled and screamed, and always through the tumult came the gruff hoot of laughter.

Said Caeltia:

'Do you know these people?'

'The woman is Eileen Ni Cooley,' replied Mary, 'for I know her walk, but I don't know the shape of the men.'

Caeltia laughed quietly to himself.

'The taller of these men,' said he, 'is the Seraph Cuchulain, the other man is that Brien O'Brien we were telling you of.'

Mary's face flamed, but she made no remark.

In a few minutes these people drew near.

Eileen Ni Cooley was dishevelled. Her shawl hung only from one shoulder and there were holes in it, her dress was tattered, and a long wisp of red hair streamed behind her like a flame. Her face was red also, and her eyes were anxious as they roved from one to the other.

She came directly to the girl and sat beside her; young Cuchulain set himself down beside Art, but Brien O'Brien stood a few paces distant with his fists thrust in his pockets and he chewing strongly on tobacco. Every now and then he growled a harsh creak of a laugh, and then covered it ostentatiously with his hand.

'God be with you, Mary Ni Cahan,' said Eileen Ni Cooley, and she twisted up her flying hair and arranged her shawl.

'What's wrong with you?' said Mary.

'Where's your father?' said Eileen.

'I don't know where he is. When we lifted from sleep a morning ago he wasn't in his place, and we haven't seen him since that time.'

'What am I going to do at all?' said Eileen in a low voice. 'These men have me tormented the way I don't know how to manage.'

'What could my father do?' said Mary sternly, 'and you playing tricks on him since the day you were born.'

150

'That's between myself and him,' replied Eileen, 'and it doesn't matter at all. I wanted your father to beat O'Brien for me, for he won't leave me alone day or night, and I can't get away from him.'

Mary leaned to her whispering:

'My father couldn't beat that man, for I saw the two of them fighting on the Donnybrook Road, and he had no chance against him.'

'He could beat him, indeed,' said Eileen indignantly, 'and I'd give him good help myself.'

'If my father owes you anything,' said Mary, 'I'm ready to pay it for him, so let us both rise against the man, and maybe the pair of us would make him fly.'

Eileen stared at her.

'I hit him once,' continued Mary, 'and I would like well to hit him again; my people here would keep his friend from joining against us.'

The blue eyes of Eileen Ni Cooley shone with contentment; she slipped the shawl from her shoulders and let it drop to the ground.

'We'll do that, Mary,' said she, 'and let us do it now.'

So the women lifted to their feet and they walked towards Brien O'Brien, and suddenly they leaped on him like a pair of panthers, and they leaped so suddenly that he went down against the road with a great bump.

But he did not stay down.

He rose after one dumbfounded moment, and he played with the pair of them the way a conjurer would play with two balls, so that the breath went out of their bodies, and they had to sit down or suffocate.

'That's the kind of man he is,' panted Eileen.

'Very well!' said Mary fiercely, 'we'll try him again in a minute.'

The camp was in confusion, and from that confusion Art leaped towards Brien O'Brien, but the Seraph Cuchulain

151

leaped and outleaped Art, and set himself bristling by the elbow of his friend; then Caeltia, with his face shining happily, tiptoed forward and ranged with Art against these two, but Finaun went quicker than they all; he leaped between the couples, and there was not a man of the four dared move against his hand.

In a second that storm blew itself out, and they returned to their seats smiling foolishly.

'Let the women be quiet,' said Brien O'Brien harshly.

He also seated himself with his back touching against the donkey's legs.

The ass had finished eating and drinking, and was now searching the horizon with the intent eye of one who does not see anything, but only looks on the world without in order to focus steadily the world within.

Brien O'Brien stared with a new interest at Finaun, and revolved his quid. Said he to Cuchulain:

'Would the old lad be able to treat us the way Rhadamanthus did, do you think?'

'He could do that,' laughed Cuchulain, 'and he could do it easily.'

O'Brien moved the quid to the other side of his jaw.

'If he slung us out of this place we wouldn't know where we might land,' said he.

'That is so,' replied Cuchulain, thrusting a sleek curl between his teeth. 'I don't know these regions, and I don't know where we might land, or if we would ever land. Only for that I would go against him,' and he waggled his finger comically at Finaun.

Art commenced to snigger and Finaun laughed heartily, but Caeltia eyed Cuchulain so menacingly that the seraph kept a quiet regard on him for the rest of the day.

Peace was restored, and while they were revolving peace and wondering how to express it, Patsy Mac Cann came on them from a side path that ran narrowly between small hills.

CHAPTER XXX

WHEN Mac Cann saw the visitors he halted for an instant and then came forward very slowly, with his head on one side and his thumb rasping steadily on his chin.

He was staring at Brien O'Brien, and as he stared he bristled like a dog.

'It's the man himself,' said he, 'the man that stole my clothes.'

O'Brien peeped upwards at him but did not move.

'Sit down and hold your prate,' said he, 'or I'll steal your life.'

Mac Cann would have thrown himself on his enemy, but at that moment he caught sight of Eileen Ni Cooley and her face drove the other out of his head.

He stared.

'It's yourself!' said he.

'It is me, sure enough, Padraig.'

'You'll be going away in a minute, I suppose,' said he grimly.

He sat on the grass and there was peace once more. He was sitting beside O'Brien, and the ass was still thinking deeply with his hocks touching against their shoulder-blades.

When he seated himself they were all silent, for, in face of everything, Mac Cann took the lead, and they waited for him to speak.

O'Brien was looking at him sideways with a grin on his hard jaw. He creaked out a little laugh, and then covered it up with his hand as one who was abashed, but Mac Cann paid no attention to him.

His attention was on Eileen Ni Cooley.

'You're a great woman,' said he, 'and you're full of fun surely.'

'I'm everything you like to call me,' replied Eileen.

'Which of the men are you with this time, or are you travelling with the pair of them?'

'I don't want either of them, Padraig, but I can't get away from them anyhow. They won't let me go my own road, and they're marching at my elbows for two days and two nights, cursing and kicking and making a noise every step of the way.'

'They're doing that!' said Patsy.

'They are doing that, Padraig. It's O'Brien is the worst, for the other fellow is only helping him and doesn't care for me at all. Catching me they do be, and holding me ...'

'Aye!' said Patsy.

'I can't get away from O'Brien,' said she, 'and I thought that if I could find yourself——'

'You were looking for me?'

'I was looking for you this time, Padraig.'

'Aye!' said Patsy, and he turned a black eye on Brien O'Brien, and his eye looked like a little, hard ball of stone.

'You'll be left alone from this day out,' said Patsy.

'Mind yourself!' growled Brien O'Brien. 'Mind yourself, my hardy man, or you'll waken up among the spooks.'

Patsy held him with that solid eye.

'Spooks!' said he, and suddenly he rolled on top of Brien O'Brien, his left hand grabbing at the throat, his right fist jabbing viciously with packed knuckles.

Down went Brien O'Brien's head and up went his heels; then he gave a mighty wriggle and started to come up, his hands threshing like the wings of a mill. As he came up they rolled, and now Mac Cann was below; but Brien O'Brien's head had disturbed the donkey, and, without emerging from cogitation, the ass let his two heels fly at the enemy of thought behind him; Patsy saw for an instant the white flash of those

154

little hoofs across his face, but Brien of the O'Brien Nation took them full on his forehead and his brows cracked in like the shell of an egg; he relaxed, he sagged, he drooped and huddled limply to Patsy's bosom, and for three seconds Mac Cann lay quietly beneath him, captured by astonishment.

The donkey had again related the infinity without to the eternity within, and his little hoofs were as peaceful as his mild eye.

Mac Cann tugged himself from beneath that weighty carcass and came to his feet.

Mary and Eileen were both sitting rigid, with arms at full stretch and their fingers tipping straitly on the ground, while their round eyes were wide in an unwinking stare.

Caeltia was on his feet and was crouching at an equally crouching Cuchulain. Patsy saw the curl jerking as the lips of the seraph laughed.

Art was frozen on one knee in the mid-act of rising, and Finaun was combing his beard while he looked fixedly at Eileen Ni Cooley.

Twenty seconds only had elapsed since Mac Cann rolled sideways on Brien O'Brien.

The Seraph Cuchulain was staring under Caeltia's arm. He blew the golden curl from his lips and sounded a laugh that was like the ringing of silver bells.

'What will Rhadamanthus say this time?' quoth he, and with that he turned and tripped happily down the road and away.

Mac Cann regarded the corpse.

'We had better bury the man,' said he gloomily.

He took a short spade from the cart, and with it he made a hole in the roadside.

They laid Brien O'Brien in that hole.

'Wait for a minute,' said Mac Cann. 'It's not decent to send him off that way.'

He pushed a hand into his pocket and pulled it out again with money in it.

'He should have something with himself and he taking the long journey.'

He lifted O'Brien's clenched fist, forced it open, and put a silver threepenny-piece into it; then he tightened the pale hand again and folded it with the other on his breast.

They wrapped a newspaper about his face, and they threw the clay over Brien of the O'Brien Nation and stamped it down well with their feet; and as they left him the twilight stole over the land, and a broad star looked peacefully down through the grey distances.

CHAPTER XXXI

THEY walked through the evening.

Dusk had fallen and in the drowsy half-lights the world stretched itself in peacefulness.

They had come to a flat country that whispered in grass; there were no more of the little hills that roll and fall and roll; there were scarcely any trees; here and there in great space a beech swung its slow boughs and made a quiet noise in the stillness; here and there a stiff tree lifted its lonely greenness, and around it the vast horizon stretched away and away to sightlessness.

There was silence here, there was deep silence, and over all the dusk drowsed and folded and increased.

With what slow veils the darkness deepened! the gentle weaver spun her thin webs and drooped soft coverings from the sky to the clay; momently the stars came flashing their tiny signals, gathering their bright hosts by lonely clusters, and one thin sickle of the moon grew from a cloud and stood distantly as a sign of gold.

But the quiet beauty of the heavens and the quiet falling to sleep of the earth had for this night no effect on one of our travellers.

Mac Cann was ill at ease. He was moody and irritable, and he moved from Eileen Ni Cooley to his daughter and back again to Eileen Ni Cooley, and could not content himself with either of them.

The angels were treading at the rear of the cart talking among themselves; the slow drone of their voices drifted up the road, and from this murmuring the words God and Beauty and Love would detach themselves and sing recurringly on the air like incantations.

Eileen Ni Cooley trod on the left side of the ass. She trod like a featureless shade; her shawl wrapped blottingly about her face and her mind moving within herself and for herself.

Mac Cann and his daughter went together by the right side of the donkey, and, as he looked constantly at his daughter, his eyes were furtive and cunning.

He tapped her elbow:

'Mary,' he whispered, 'I want to talk to you.'

She replied in a voice that was low from his contact:

'I want to talk to yourself,' said she.

'What do you want to say?'

'I want to know where you got the money that I saw in your hand when you buried the man?'

'That's what I'm going to tell you about,' he whispered. 'Be listening to me now and don't make any noise.'

'I'm listening to you,' said Mary.

'What have we got to do with these lads behind us?' said Patsy urgently. 'They are nothing to us at all, and I'm tired of them.'

'There's a thing to say!' quoth she.

'This is what we'll do. To-night we won't unyoke the ass, and when they are well asleep we'll walk quietly off with ourselves and leave them there. Eileen Ni Cooley will come with us, and in the morning we'll be distant.'

'I won't do that,' said Mary.

He darted at her a sparkle of rage.

'You'll do what I say, you strap, or it'll be the worse for you!' said his violent whisper.

'I won't do that,' she hissed, 'and I tell you I won't.'

'By the living Jingo . . .!' said Patsy.

She came at him whispering with equal fierceness.

'What have you done on the men?' said she. 'What did you do on them that you want to run away from them in the night?'

'Keep your tongue in your teeth, you——!'

'Where were you for a day and a half? Where did you get the money from that I saw in your hand when you buried the man?'

Patsy composed himself with difficulty; he licked his dry lips.

'There's no fooling you, alannah, and I'll tell you the truth.'

He glanced cautiously to where the others were coming deep in talk.

'This is what I did. I went to that place by Ard-Martin where we buried the things, and I dug them up.'

'Oh!' said Mary.

'I dug them up, and I took them away, and I sold them to a man for money.'

'Oh!' said Mary.

'They're sold, do you hear? And there's no going back on it; so do what I tell you about the ass this night, and we'll take our own road from now on.'

'I won't do it,' whispered Mary, and she was almost speechless with rage.

Mac Cann thrust his face close to hers, grinning like a madman.

'You won't do it!' said he. 'What will you do then against your father?'

'I'll go on to the place with the men,' she stammered.

'You'll come with me this night.'

'I'll not go,' said she harshly.

'You'll come with me this night,' said he.

'I'll not go,' she screamed at him.

At the sound of her scream everybody came running to them.

'Is there anything wrong?' said Art.

'She's only laughing at a joke I told her,' said Patsy. 'Make that ass go on, Mary a grah, for it's walking as if it was going asleep.'

Caeltia was looking at Mac Cann so fixedly, with such a severe gravity of eye, that the blood of the man turned to water and he could scarcely hold himself upright. For the first time in his life Mac Cann knew what fear was.

'To-morrow,' said Caeltia, 'we will be going away from you; let us be peaceful then for our last night together.'

'Aye,' said Patsy, 'let us be comfortable for this night of all nights.'

He turned away, and with a great effort at carelessness he moved to the donkey's head.

'Come on, Mary,' said he.

Eileen Ni Cooley trod beside him for a moment.

'What's wrong with you, Padraig?' said she.

'Nothing at all, Eileen; just leave me alone for a minute, for I want to talk to the girl.'

'You can count on me for any thing, Padraig.'

'I don't know whether I can or not,' he muttered savagely. 'Keep quiet for ten minutes in the name of God.'

For a few dull seconds they paced in quiet. Patsy moistened his lips with his tongue.

'What are you going to do, Mary?'

'I don't know,' she replied. 'What man did you sell the things to?'

'I sold them to a man that lives near by—a rich man in a big house.'

'There's only one big house about here.'

'That's the house.'

She was silent.

'If you're going to tell the men,' said her father, 'give me two hours' law this night until I get away, and then you can tell them and be damned to you.'

'Listen to me!' said the girl.

'I'm listening.'

'There is only one thing to be done, and it has got to be done at once: go you to the place of that rich man and take the things away from his house, and bury them back again in the place they were buried. If you want any help I'll go with you myself.'

Mac Cann's thumb wandered to his chin, and a sound as of filing was heard while he rubbed it. His voice was quite changed as he replied:

'Begor!' said he.

'You're full of fun,' said he thoughtfully. He covered his mouth with his hand then and stared thoughtfully down the road.

'Will you do that?' said Mary.

He thumped a hand heavily on her shoulder.

'I will so, and I do wonder that I didn't think of it myself, for it's the thing that ought to be done.'

And now as they marched the atmosphere had changed; there was once more peace or the precursor of it; from Mac Cann a tempered happiness radiated as of old: he looked abroad without misgiving, and he looked at his daughter with the cynical kindliness habitual to him. They trod so for a little time arranging their thoughts, then:

'We are near enough to that house to be far enough from it if there's any reason to be far,' said Mac Cann, 'so this is what I say, let us stop where we are for the night, and in the morning we'll go on from here.'

'Very well,' said Mary, 'let us stop here.'

Her father drew the ass to the side of the road and there halted it.

'We'll go to bed now,' he shouted to the company, and they all agreed to that.

'I'm going to unyoke the beast,' said Mary, with a steady eye on her father.

He replied heartily:

'Why wouldn't you do that? Let him out to get something to eat like the rest of us.'

'There isn't any water,' he complained a minute later.

'What will that animal do? and what will we do ourselves?'

'I have two big bottles of water in the cart,' said Mary.

'And I have a little bottle in my pocket,' said he, 'so we're all right.'

The donkey was unyoked, and he went at once to stand with his feet in the wet grass. He remained so for a long time without eating, but he did eat when that idea occurred to him.

The brazier was lit, the sacks strewn on the ground, and they sat about the fire in their accustomed places and ate their food. After a smoke and a little conversation each person stretched backwards, covering themselves with other sacks, and they went heartily to sleep.

'We will have to be up early in the morning,' was Patsy's last remark, 'for you are in a hurry to get back your things,' and saying so he stretched his length with the others.

When a still hour had drifted by Mary raised cautiously and tiptoed to her father. As she stood by him he slid the sacks aside and came to his feet, and they moved a little way down the road.

'Now,' said Mary, 'you can do what you said you'd do.'

'I'll do that,' said he.

'And get back as quick as you can.'

'It's a distance there and back again. I'll be here in the morning, but I'll be late.'

'Bury the things the way they were before.'

'That's all right,' and he moved a step backwards.

'Father!' said Mary softly.

He returned to her.

'What more do you want?' said he impatiently.

She put her arms about his neck.

'What the devil are you doing?' said he in astonishment, and he tried to wriggle loose from her.

But she did not say another word, and after a moment he

162

put his own arms about her with a grunt and held her tightly.

'I'm away now,' said he, and, moving against the darkness, he disappeared.

For half a minute the sound of his feet was heard, and then the darkness covered him.

Mary returned to her place by the brazier. She stretched close to Eileen Ni Cooley and lay staring at the moving clouds.

In a few minutes she was asleep, although she had not felt any heaviness on her eyes.

CHAPTER XXXII

No one was awake.

In the brazier a faint glow peeped from the white turf-ash;
the earth seemed to be holding its breath, so still it was; the
clouds hung immovably each in its place; a solitary tree near
by folded its wide limbs into the darkness and made no
sound.

Nothing stirred in the world but the ass as he lifted his
head slowly and drooped it again; his feet were sunken in a
plot of grass and he was quiet as the earth.

Then I came softly, and I spoke to the ass in the darkness.

'Little ass,' quoth I, 'how is everything with you?'

'Everything is very well,' said the ass.

'Little ass,' said I, 'tell me what you do be thinking of
when you fix your eye on vacancy and stare there for a long
time?'

'I do be thinking,' said the ass, 'of my companions, and
sometimes I do be looking at them.'

'Who are your companions?'

'Last night I saw the Cyclops striding across a hill; there
were forty of them, and each man was forty feet high; they
had only one eye in their heads and they looked through
that; they looked through it the way a fire stares through a
hole and they could see well.'

'How do you know they could see well?'

'One of them saw me and he called out to the others; they
did not wait, but he waited for a moment; he took me in his
arms and he stroked my head; then he put me on the ground
and went away, and in ten strides he crossed over the
mountain.'

'That was a good sight to see!'

'That was a good sight.'

'Tell me something else you saw.'

'I saw seven girls in a meadow and they were playing together; when they were tired playing they lay on the grass and they went to sleep; I drew near and stretched beside them on the grass, and I watched them for a long time; but when they awakened they disappeared into the air and were gone like puffs of smoke.

'I saw the fairy host marching through a valley in the hills; wide, silken banners were flying above their heads; some had long swords in their hands and some had musical instruments, and there were others who carried a golden apple in their hands, and others again with silver lilies and cups of heavy silver; they were beautiful and proud and they marched courageously; they marched past me for three gay hours while I stood on the slope of a hill.

'I saw three centaurs riding out of a wood; they raced round and round me shouting and waving their hands; one of them leaned his elbows on my back, and they talked of a place in the middle of a forest; they pelted me with tufts of grass; then they went by a narrow path into the wood, and they rode away.

'I saw a herd of wild asses in a plain; men were creeping around them in the long grass, but the asses ran suddenly, and they killed the men with their hoofs and their teeth; I galloped in the middle of them for half a night, but I remembered Mary Ni Cahan, and when I remembered her I turned from all my companions and I galloped home again.'

'Those were all good sights to see!'

'They were all good sights.'

'Good-bye, little ass,' said I.

'Good-bye, you,' said he.

He lay along the grass then and he closed his eyes, but I

turned back and crouched by the brazier, watching the people while they slept, and staring often into the darkness to see did anything stir before the light came.

CHAPTER XXXIII

MAC CANN strode through the darkness for a little time, but when he found himself at sufficient distance from the camp he began to run.

There was not very much time wherein to do all that he had engaged before the morning dawned, and so he took to this mode of activity which was not one for which he had any reverence. He was a heavy man and did not run with either grace or ease, but he could hasten his movements to a jog-trot, and, as his physical condition was perfect, he could continue such a trot until hunger brought it to a halt, for he was never fatigued, being as strong and tireless as a bear.

He was the most simple-minded of men. When he was engaged in one affair he could not meddle with anything else, and now that he was running he could do nothing but run—he could not think, for instance. When it was necessary to think he would either walk very slowly or stand stock-still, and then he would think with great speed and with great simplicity. His head bade his legs be quiet while it was occupied, and, when they were in motion, his legs tramped hush to his head, which obeyed instantly; and he was so well organised on these lines that there was never any quarrel between the extremities.

It was, therefore, the emptiest of men that now pounded the road. He would deal with an emergency when it was visible, but until then he snapped a finger and forgot it, for he had learned that the first word of an emergency is a warning, the second a direction for escape, its third utterance is in action, and it will only be waited for by a fool.

Exactly what he would do when he arrived at the house he

did not know, and as yet he made no effort to deal with that problem: he obeyed the prime logical necessity, which was to get there: once there and the second step would push itself against him, and from that cause the most orderly of results would ensue. If there was no trouble he would succeed in his enterprise; if there was trouble he would fly—that was his simple programme.

And meantime there was nothing in the world but darkness and the rhythmic tramping of his feet. These, with a faintly hushing wind, kept his ears occupied. He had much of the cat's facility for seeing in the dark, and he had the sense of direction which some birds have, so he made good progress.

After half an hour's steady movement he came to the house for which he was seeking, and halted there.

It was a long, low building, standing back from the road. There was a stone wall around this house, and the entrance was by an iron gate.

Mac Cann touched the gate, for experience had taught him that gates are not always locked, but this one was locked securely. By the gate was a caretaker's lodge, so he moved quietly from that place and walked by the wall.

There was glass on the top of the wall, which halted him for a few moments while he sucked his incautious hand. To cope with this he gathered several large stones and placed them on top of each other, and he stood on these; then he threw his coat and waistcoat over the glass and climbed easily across.

He was in a shrubbery. About him every few paces were short, stiff bushes, some of which were armed with spines, which did their duty on his hands and the legs of his trousers; but he regarded these with an inattention which must have disgusted them. He tiptoed among these guardians and was shortly free of them and on a gravel pathway. Crossing this he came on quiet flower-beds which he skirted: the house was now visible as a dark mass distant some hundred yards.

Saving for one window the place was entirely dark, and it was towards that window he directed his careful steps.

'It's better to look at something than at nothing,' quoth he.

He was again on a gravel path, and the stones tried to crunch and wriggle under his feet, but he did not allow that to happen.

He came to the window and, standing well to the side, peeped in.

He saw a square room furnished as a library. The entire section of the walls which he could spy was covered from floor to ceiling with books. There were volumes of every size, every shape, every colour. There were long, narrow books that held themselves like grenadiers at stiff attention. There were short, fat books that stood solidly like aldermen who were going to make speeches and were ashamed but not frightened. There were mediocre books bearing themselves with the carelessness of folk who are never looked at and have consequently no shyness. There were solemn books that seemed to be feeling for their spectacles; and there were tattered, important books that had got dirty because they took snuff, and were tattered because they had been crossed in love and had never married afterwards. There were prim, ancient tomes that were certainly ashamed of their heroines and utterly unable to obtain a divorce from the hussies; and there were lean, rakish volumes that leaned carelessly, or perhaps it was with studied elegance, against their neighbours, murmuring in affected tones, 'All heroines are charming to us.'

In the centre of the room was a heavy, black table, and upon the highly polished surface of this a yellow light fell from globes on the ceiling.

At this table a man was seated, and he was staring at his

hands. He was a man of about thirty years of age. A tall, slender man with a lean face, and, to Patsy, he was of an appalling cleanliness—a cleanliness really to make one shudder: he was shaved to the last closeness; he was washed to the ultimate rub; on him both soap and water had wrought their utmost, and could have no further ambitions; his wristlets gleamed like snow on a tree, and his collar rose upon a black coat as the plumage of a swan emerges spotlessly from water.

His cleanliness was a sight to terrify any tramp, but it only angered Mac Cann, who was not liable to terror of anything but hunger.

'I would like to give you a thump on the head, you dirty dog!' said Patsy, breathing fiercely against the corner of the window-pane, and his use of the adjective was singular as showing in what strange ways extremes can meet.

This was the man to whom he had sold the gear of his companions: an indelicate business indeed, and one which the cleanliness of the purchaser assisted him to rectify, and it was in this room that the barter had been conducted. By craning his neck a little he could see an oaken settle, and upon this his sacks were lying with their mouths open and the gleaming cloths flooding at the entry.

While he stared, the man removed his fingers from his eyes and put them in his pocket; then he arose very slowly and paced thoughtfully towards the window.

Mac Cann immediately ducked beneath the window-ledge. He heard the window opened, and knew the man was leaning his elbows on the sill while he stared into the darkness.

'Begor!' said Patsy to himself, and he flattened his body against the wall.

After a time, which felt longer than it could have been, he heard the man moving away, and he then popped up and again peeped through the window.

The man had opened the door of the room which faced the window and was standing in the entry. Now his hands were clasped behind his back, his head was sunken forward, and he seemed to be looking at his feet, which is the habit of many men when they think, for when the eyes touch the feet a circuit is formed and one's entire body is able to think at ease.

Suddenly the man stepped into a black corridor and he disappeared. Mac Cann heard about ten steps ringing from a solid flooring, then he heard a door open and shut, then he heard nothing but the shifting and rubbing of his own clothes and the sound his own nose made when he breathed outwards: there was a leathern belt about his middle, and from the noise which it made one would have fancied that it was woven of thunders—there was a great silence; the lighted room was both inviting and terrifying, for it was even more silent than the world outside; the steady globes stared at the window like the eyes of a mad fish, and one could imagine that the room had pricked up invisible ears and was listening towards the window, and one could imagine also that the room would squeak and wail if any person were to come through anywhere but a door and stand in it.

Mac Cann did not imagine any of these things. He spat on his hands, and in the twinkling of an eye he was inside the window. In three long and hasty paces he placed a hand on each of the sacks, and just as he gripped them he heard a door opening, and he heard the footsteps ringing again on a solid flooring.

'I'm in,' said he viciously, 'and I won't go out.'

His eyes blinked around like the flash of lightning, but there was no place to hide. He stepped across the oaken chest and crouched down. Behind him, from the floor upwards, were books, in front was the big chest, and on top of it the two bulging sacks. He was well screened and he could peep between the sacks.

He stared towards the door.

The clean man came in and stood aside. Following him came a woman who was, if anything, more rigorously washed than he was. Somehow, although she was a tall woman, she seemed as light as a feather. She was clad in a delicate pink gown of such gossamer quality that it balanced and swam on the air with every movement she made. Across her bare shoulders was a lawn veiling, which also sailed and billowed as she moved. Her hair seemed to be of the finest spun gold, light as thistle-down, and it, too, waved and floated in little strands and ringlets.

These two people sat down at different sides of the table, and for a time they did not speak to each other. Then the man raised his head:

'I got a letter from your mother this morning,' said he in a low voice.

The woman answered him in a tone that was equally low:

'I did not know you corresponded with her.'

The man made a slight gesture:

'Nor did I know that your correspondence was as peculiar as I have found it,' said he.

Said the woman coldly:

'You are opening this subject again.'

'I am: I have to: your mother confirms everything that I have charged you with.'

'My mother hates me,' said the woman; 'she would confirm anything that was said of me, if it was bad enough.'

'She is your mother.'

'Oh no, she is not! When I ceased to be a child she ceased to be a mother. We are only two women who are so well acquainted that we can be enemies without any shame of each other.'

'Are you not talking nonsense?'

'I have committed a crime against her. She will never forgive me for being younger than she is, and for being pretty in her own fashion. She left my father because he said I was good-looking.'

'All that ...!' said the man, with a movement of his shoulder.

'As to what she would do against me, you should know it well enough, considering the things she told you before we were married.'

'You admitted that they were not all lies.'

'Some of the facts were true, all of the colouring was false—they are the things a loving mother says about her daughter! but that is an old story now, or I had fancied so.'

'One forgets the old story until the new story drags it to memory,' said he.

She also moved her shoulders slightly:

'I begin to find these conversations tiresome.'

'I can understand that. ... With her letter your mother enclosed some other letters from her friends—they insist on the facts, and add others.'

'Are they letters, or copies of letters?'

'They are copies.'

'Of course my mother has forbidden you to disclose the fact that she forwarded her friends' private correspondence to you.'

'Naturally.'

'Very naturally; the reason being that she wrote these letters herself to herself. There are no originals of these copies.'

'Again you are talking nonsense.'

'I know her better than you do, better than she knows herself.'

There was silence between them again for a few moments, and again it was broken by the man.

'There are some things I cannot do,' said he, and paused: 'I cannot search in unclean places for unclean information,' he continued, and again the silence fell between these two people.

She could bear that silence, but he could not:

'You do not say anything!' said he.

'This seems to be so entirely your business,' was her quiet reply.

He moved a hand at that:

'You cannot divorce yourself from me with such ease. This is our business, and we must settle it between us.'

Her hand was resting on the table, and suddenly he reached to her and laid his own hand on hers. She did not withdraw, but the stiffening of her body was more than withdrawal. He drew his hand away again.

'We are reasonable creatures and must question our difficulties,' said he gently, 'we must even help each other to resolve them.'

'These difficulties are not of my making.'

'They are, and you are lying to me shamelessly.'

Again between these people a silence fell which was profound but not quiet. That soundlessness was tingling with sound; there were screams latent in it; it was atrocious and terrifying. The man's hand was pressed against his forehead and his eyes were closed, but what he was looking at was known only to himself in the silence of his being. The woman sat upright an arm's-length from him, and although her eyes were wide and calm, she also was regarding that which was free within herself, and very visible to her.

'There are things I cannot do,' said the man, emerging as with an effort from subterranean caves and secret prospects. He continued speaking, calmly but tonelessly:

'I have striven to make a rule of life for myself and to follow it, but I have not sought to impose my laws on any one else—not on you, certainly. Still there are elementary duties which we owe to one another and which cannot be

174

renounced by either of us. There is a personal, I might say, a domestic loyalty expected by each of us. . . .'

'I expect nothing,' said she.

'I exact nothing,' said the man, 'but I expect that—I expect it as I expect air for my lungs and stability under my feet. You must not withdraw that from me. You are not the individual you think; you are a member of society, and you live by it; you are a member of my household, and you live by it.'

She turned her face to him but not her eyes.

'I do not ask anything from you,' said she, 'and I have accepted as little as was possible.'

He clenched his hand on the table, but when he spoke his voice was without emphasis:

'That is part of my grievance against you. Life is to give and take without any weighing of the gifts. You will do neither, and yet our circumstances are such that we must accommodate each other whether we will or not.

'I am an exact man,' he continued; 'perhaps you find that trying, but I cannot live in doubt. Whatever happens to hinder or assist my consciousness must be known to me. It is a law of my being: it is my ancestral heritage, and I have no command over it.'

'I also,' said she coldly, 'am an heir of the ages, and must take my bequests whether I like them or not.'

'I love you,' said the man, 'and I have proved it many times. I am not demonstrative, and I am shy of this fashion of speech. Perhaps that shyness of speech is responsible for more than is apparent to either of us in a world eager for speech and gesture, but I say the word now in all sincerity, with a gravity, perhaps, which you find repulsive. Be at least as honest with me no matter how cruel you are. I cannot live in the half-knowledge which is jealousy. It tears my heart. It makes me unfit for thought, for life, for sleep, even for death. I must know, or I am a madman and no man any longer, a wild beast that will bite itself in despair of hurting its enemy.'

The woman's tongue slipped over her pale lips in a quick, red flash.

'Have you anything to say to me?' said he.

There was no reply.

He insisted:

'Are the statements in your mother's letter true?'

'My mother's letter!' said she.

'Have I reason for this jealousy?' he breathed.

Her reply was also but a breathing:

'I will not tell you anything,' said she.

Once again the silence drowsed and droned between the two people, and again they repaired to the secret places of their souls where energy was sucked from them until they existed only in a torpor. The woman rose languidly from her chair, and, after an instant, the man stood also.

Said he:

'I will leave here in the morning.'

'You will let me see the boy,' she murmured.

'If,' said he, 'I ever learn that you have spoken to the boy I will kill you, and I will kill the boy.'

The woman went out then, and her feet tapped lightly along the corridor. The man turned down the lights in the yellow globes and stepped to the door; his footsteps also died away in the darkness, but in a different direction.

Mac Cann stood up:

'Begor!' said he, stretching his cramped knees.

About him was a great darkness and a great silence, and the air of that room was more unpleasant than any atmosphere he had ever breathed. But he had the nerves of a bear and a resolute adherence to his own business, so the excitement of another person could only disturb him for a moment. Still, he did not like the room, and he made all haste to get out of it.

He lifted the sacks, stepped carefully to the window, and dropped them out. Then he climbed through and picked them up.

In five minutes he was on the road again. Along it for some dozen yards he trod like a great cat until he had left the gate-keeper's lodge well behind him; then, with the sacks across his shoulders, he took to the steady jog-trot which was to last for about three hours.

CHAPTER XXXIV

MARY awakened early.

The morning was grey and the sky flat and solid, with here and there thin furrows marking its gathered fields.

She raised her head, and looked towards her father's place, but he was not there, and the sacks were crumpled on the ground.

Finaun's great length was lying along the ground, and he was straight as a rod. Caeltia was curved a little, and one hand was flung above his head. Art was rolled up like a ball; his hands were gripped about his knees, and he had kicked the sacks off his body. Eileen Ni Cooley had her two arms under her face; she was lying on her breast, and her hair streamed sidewards from her head along the dull grass.

As Mary lay back, for it was still too early to rise, a thought came to her and she rose to her feet again. She thought that perhaps her father had come softly in the night and moved the ass and cart away with him, and that thought lifted her breast in panic.

She ran down the road and saw the cart with its shafts poked in the air, and further away the donkey was lying on his side.

She came back on tiptoe smiling happily to herself, and, with infinite precaution, she restored the sacks to Art's body and composed herself again to sleep. She did not raise the camp, for she wished to give her father all possible time so that he might return unnoticed.

And while she slept the sky unpacked its locked courses; the great galleons of cloud went sailing to the west, and thus, fleet by fleet, relieved those crowded harbours. The black cloud-masses went rolling on the sky—They grew together, touched and swung apart and slipped away with heavy haste, as when down narrow waters an armada weighs, filling listlessly her noisy sails, while the slender spars are hauled to the breeze; the watchmen stand at the posts, and the fenders are still hung from the pitching sides; almost the vessels touch; the shipmen shout as they bear heavily on their oaken poles; and then they swing again, the great prows bear away, the waters boil between, and the loud farewells sing faintly to the waves.

And now the sky was a bright sea sown with islands; they shrank and crumbled and drifted away, islands no more, but a multitude of plumes and flakes and smoky wreaths hastily scudding, for the sun had lifted his tranquil eye on the heavens; he stared afar down the grey spaces, and before his gaze the mists went huddling and hiding in lovely haste; the dark spaces became white, the dark blue spaces became light blue, and earth and sky sparkled and shone in his radiant beam.

The camp awakened before Mary did, and again the enquiry went as to the whereabouts of her father:

'He will be here shortly,' said Mary. 'He must have gone along the road to see if there was anything he could find for us to eat'; and she delayed the preparation of their breakfast to the last possible moment. She spilled a pot of boiling water to that end, and she overturned the brazier when the water boiled again.

They were about sitting to their food when Mac Cann came in sight, and she held the meal until his arrival with his hat far to the back of his head, the happiest of smiles on his face, and a newspaper bundle in his hand.

Mary gave him a look of quick meaning:

'Were you able to find anything for the breakfast?' said she, and then she was astonished.

'I was indeed,' he replied, and he handed her the bulky newspaper package.

She used that occasion to whisper to him:

'Well?'

'That's all right,' said he, nodding at the bundle, but really in answer to her query.

She opened the parcel.

There were slices of bacon in it and slices of beef; there were ten sausages in it and the biggest half of a loaf—these, with a small flat bottle full of rum and two pairs of stockings, made up the parcel.

'Put the sausages in a pan,' said Patsy, 'and share them round and we'll eat them.'

Mary did put them on the pan, and when they were cooked she shared them round, and they were fairly eaten.

After breakfast the pipes were lit, but they rose almost immediately to continue the journey.

'This evening,' said Finaun, 'we will be saying good-bye.'

'Aye,' said Mac Cann, 'I'm sorry you're going, for we had a good time together.'

The ass took his instructions, and they went down the road. Their places were now as they had always been— Finaun and Eileen Ni Cooley and Mary Mac Cann went with the ass, and there was no lack of conversation in that assembly, for sometimes they talked to one another and sometimes they talked to the ass, but the donkey listened no matter who was being talked to, and not a person objected to him.

Patsy and Caeltia marched sturdily at the tailboard, and they were close in talk.

Behind them Art was ranging aimlessly, and lilting snatches of song. He did not know the entire of any song but he knew verses of many, and he was able to relate the tunes of these so harmoniously, with such gradual slipping of theme into theme, that twenty minutes of his varied lilting could appear like one consecutive piece of music.

'That lad has a great ear,' said Patsy. 'He could make his fortune at the music.'

'He is a musician,' Caeltia replied. 'That is his business when we are in our own place, and, as you can see, it is his pleasure also.'

Patsy was in high spirits. Now that he had successfully undone that which he had done, a real weight had lifted from him. But the thing was still so near that he could not get easily from it. His head was full of the adventures of the last few days, and although he could not speak of them he could touch them, sound them, lift the lid of his mystery and snap it to again, chuckling meanwhile to himself that those who were concerned did not know what he was talking about, and yet he was talking to himself, or to one cognisant, in hardy, adequate symbol. A puerile game for a person whose youth had been left behind for twenty years, but one which is often played nevertheless and by the most solemn minds.

It was with an impish carelessness that he addressed Caeltia:

'It won't be long before we are there,' said he.

'That is so,' was the reply.

'You'll be feeling fine, I'm thinking, when you get your own clothes on again.'

'I have not missed them very much.'

'I hope your wings and your grand gear will be all right.'

'Why should you doubt it?' returned the seraph.

'What,' said Patsy, 'if they were robbed on you! You'd be rightly in the cart, mister, if that happened.'

Caeltia puffed quietly at his pipe.

'They were robbed,' said he.

'Eh!' cried Mac Cann sharply.

The seraph turned to him, his eyes brimming with laughter.

'Aye, indeed,' said he.

Mac Cann was silent for a few seconds, but he did not dare to be silent any longer.

'You're full of fun,' said he sourly. 'What are you talking about at all?'

'Finaun and I knew all about it,' said Caeltia, 'and we were wondering what would be done by the person.'

'What did he do?' said Patsy angrily.

Caeltia returned the pipe to his mouth.

'He put them back,' said he.

'Only for that,' he continued, 'we might have had to recover them ourselves.'

'Would you have been able to get them back?' said Mac Cann humbly.

'We would have got them back; there is nothing in the world could stand against us two; there is nothing in the world could stand against one of us.'

Patsy jerked a thumb to where Art was lilting the opening bars of 'The Wind that shakes the Barley':

'Wouldn't the boy help?' said he. 'How old is the lad?'

'I don't know,' smiled Caeltia. 'He remembers more than one Day of a Great Breath, but he has no power for he has never had being, and so did not win to knowledge; he could give help for he is very strong.'

'Could you have licked Cuchulain that day?' said Patsy timidly.

'I am older than he,' replied Caeltia, 'that is to say, I am wiser than he.'

'But he was up there with yourself and could learn the tricks.'

'There is no secrecy in this world or in the others, and there are no tricks: there is Knowledge, but no person can learn more than his head is ready to welcome. That is why robbery is infantile and of no importance.'

'It fills the stomach,' replied Patsy cunningly.

'The stomach has to be filled,' said Caeltia. 'Its filling is a necessity superior to any proprietorial right or disciplinary ethic, and its problem is difficult only for children; it is filled by the air and the wind, the rain and the clay, and the tiny lives that move in the clay. There is but one property worth stealing; it is never missed by its owners, although every person who has that property offers it to all men from his gentle hands.'

'You're trying to talk like Finaun,' said Patsy gloomily.

They walked then in silence for ten minutes. Every vestige of impishness had fled from Mac Cann; he was a miserable man; his vanity was hurt and he was frightened, and this extraordinary combination of moods plunged him to a depression so profound that he could not climb therefrom without assistance.

Said Caeltia to him after a little:

'There is a thing I would like to see done, my friend.'

Mac Cann's reply came sagging as he hauled his limp ideas from those pits.

'What's that, your honour?'

'I would like to see the money thrown into this ditch as we go by.'

Patsy's depression vanished as at the glare of a torch and the trumpet of danger. He nosed the air and sniffed like a horse.

'Begor!' said he. 'You're full of——There's no sense in that,' said he sharply.

'That is what I would like to see, but everybody must act exactly as they are able to act.'

'I tell you there isn't any sense in it; give me a reasonable thing to do in the name of God and I'll do it.'

'That is the only thing I want done.'

'What's the use of making a fool of me?'

'Am I demanding anything?'

When they had walked a few paces:

'What is it, after all!' said Patsy proudly.

He thrust his hands into his pockets and exhibited them full of gold and silver.

'Just a pitch of my hand and it's gone!' said he.

'That is all,' said Caeltia. 'It's easily done.'

'So it is,' growled Patsy, and he swung his arm.

But he dropped the hand again.

'Wait a minute,' and he called Eileen Ni Cooley to his side.

'Walk with ourselves, Eileen, and don't be a stranger. There's something I want to show you.'

He opened his hand before her and it was flooding and flashing in gold.

She stared with the awe of one who looks on miracles.

'There's a great deal of money there,' she gasped.

'There's fifteen golden pounds and some shillings in it,' said Patsy, 'and here's all I care for them.'

He flung his hand then and sped the money at the full force of his shoulder.

'That's all I care for the stuff,' said he, and he gripped her arm to prevent her bounding to its recovery.

'Come on, woman dear, and leave the ha'pence alone.'

Said Caeltia:

'There is something I must throw away also, for I am getting too fond of it.'

'What's that?' said Mac Cann curiously.

'It's this pipe,' the seraph replied, and he balanced it by the mouthpiece.

'Don't throw away the good pipe,' cried Eileen Ni Cooley. 'Am I walking beside a pair of wild men this day?'

Patsy interrupted also.

'Hold on for a minute. Give me the pipe and you can take this one.' He took Caeltia's silver-mounted briar and he passed to the seraph his own blackened clay.

'You can throw that one away,' said he, and he popped Caeltia's pipe into his own mouth.

'It will do that way,' said Caeltia sadly.

He held the pipe by the stem, and with a sharp movement snapped it in halves; the head fell to the ground and a small tight wad of burning tobacco jumped from it at the shock.

'There it is,' said Caeltia.

He jerked the piece of broken stem from his hand, and after sighing deeply they marched on.

Eileen Ni Cooley was angry.

'Padraig,' said she, 'what made you throw all the golden money away, and the silver money?'

Patsy regarded her with the calm eye of a king.

'Stick your arm through mine, Eileen,' said he, 'and let us be comfortable as we go along, for the pair of us haven't had a talk for a long time, and Caeltia here wants to talk to you as well as me.'

'That is so,' said Caeltia.

Eileen did put her arm in his, and as they stepped briskly forward she stared at him with eyes that were round with admiration and astonishment.

'Aren't you the queer man, Padraig!' said she.

'I suppose,' said Patsy, 'that you'll be slipping away from us some time to-night?'

'Not if you want me to stay, Padraig.'

They opened a new conversation on that.

CHAPTER XXXV

THAT day they did not stay their travel, even to eat.

Finaun was urgent, and they ate from their hands as they marched. The ass moved his slender legs briskly, the cart rumbled, and the metals in it clashed and thumped as the wheels jolted on the rutty path.

They met no persons as they went.

From the fields near by came the fresh odour of wild grass that out-breathed again to the sun his living breath; and the sun shone, not fiercely, but kindly, tempering down the oblique ways his potent fire; above their heads and slanting away on wide wings the birds were sailing, calling a note as they went and calling again; here were trees once more; their grave shadows slept on the road, stamping the golden light with a die of ebony, and their grave voices whispered busily, quietly, like the voices of many mothers who fold against fruitful breasts the little children; so they crooned and sang, rocking their ample greenery on the air.

In the afternoon they reached the hill, close to the top of which the angels' finery was buried.

When they had ascended this hill for nearly an hour the donkey struck work.

He stood, and nothing would induce him to move further in that direction. Indeed, he slewed the cart completely round, and pointed his nose and his shafts in the direction which he considered reasonable.

They halted.

'He'll not go up there,' said Mary, and she pulled the long nose to her bosom.

'He will not,' said her father. 'Will you leave that ass

alone, Mary? Give him back his snout and behave yourself like a Christian girl.'

'You leave me alone,' said Mary; 'what harm am I doing to yourself?'

'It's that I don't like to see a woman kissing an ass.'

'Well, if you don't look at me you won't see anything.'

'You're full of fun,' said her father sternly.

He shrugged his shoulders and turned to Finaun:

'He did this once before on us and we going up a tall hill in Connaught, and although I hammered the skin off his back he wouldn't move a step; he's a great ass, mind you, mister, and maybe we ought to have looked for a gentler way up this hill.'

Finaun was feeding tufts of grass to the donkey, and the donkey was eating these with appetite.

'There is no need to come further,' said Finaun. 'We are almost in sight of the place and can make our adieus here.'

'Oh! we'll leave the beast,' cried Mac Cann, 'and we'll all go up to see the last of you.'

'It is better that we should part here,' said Finaun gently. 'We do not wish to be seen at the last.'

'You can have it your own way,' said Patsy sulkily.

Finaun stood towering over Mac Cann; he placed his hands on Patsy's shoulders and solemnly blessed him in round language, then he kissed him tenderly on either cheek.

'Begor!' said Patsy.

And Finaun did the same for Eileen Ni Cooley and for Mary, and he kissed the two of them on their cheeks; then he laid his palm on the donkey's muzzle and blessed that beast, and he strode mightily up the hill.

Caeltia advanced to Patsy, but Mac Cann was embarrassed. He had been kissed by a man, so he lit his pipe in self-defence and kept it in his mouth.

'You're going off?' said he to Caeltia, and he puffed like a chimney.

'I'm going off,' replied Caeltia in a low voice.

Patsy took the pipe from his mouth and put it into the seraph's hand.

'Here,' said he, 'take a last pull at that and ease your heart.'

Caeltia did take it, and he smoked it, and it did ease his heart.

'I'll give you the spade out of the cart,' continued Patsy, 'for you'll have to dig the things up. There it is, and it doesn't matter whether it's lost or not.'

'It is good-bye now,' said Caeltia, shouldering the spade, and he returned the pipe to Patsy, who put it instantly in his mouth.

Caeltia held out his hand, and Mac Cann put his own into it.

While their hands were together Patsy was seized with compunction—he drew the seraph aside a few paces:

'Listen!' said he. 'I played a trick on you the time I was taking the money out of my pocket to throw it away.'

'Yes?' said Caeltia.

'I let one of the gold pieces slip through my fingers, and it's lying at the bottom of my pocket at this minute, but I'll throw it away, mister honey, if you say so.'

Caeltia looked at him, and a smile of great contentment crept over his lips.

'If I were you,' said he, 'I'd keep it.'

Mac Cann nodded at him very solemnly:

'I'll keep it,' said he earnestly, 'and I'll spend it.'

Caeltia then said his adieus to the others, and he tramped up the hill with the spade balanced in his hand.

The piece of gold was burning in Patsy's pocket. He turned to Art:

'Well, young boy! there's my hand, and good luck be with you; give up racing about and climbing trees and you'll be all right; you've the makings of a good hand on you, and that's a great thing, and you've got the music.'

'Good-bye,' said Art, and they shook hands.

Eileen Ni Cooley took his hand also, then she and Patsy strode to the cart, and with the donkey they moved down the hill.

Mary stood in front of Art, and she did not look at him; she turned her grave face away, and stared sidewards where the late sunshine drowsed in gold on the rough slopes. She put her hand out to him.

He took her hand and held it between his own; he raised it to his lips, and he held it there pressing against his mouth.

He dropped it, and stood back a pace staring at her; he struck his hands together in a wild movement; he turned and ran swiftly after his companions.

These two had never spoken to each other.

Near the top of the hill he came on Finaun and Caeltia, and the three went together.

In a little they reached the point in the road where they had slept during their first night on earth, and where they had eaten their first meal on a sunny morning. Distant a few paces they saw the tree.

Caeltia dug there until he uncovered the sacks. He pulled these from the clay and opened them, and each of the angels retrieved his own belongings from the medley.

Finaun was urgent and thoughtful. He apparelled himself hastily, while, with less speed, Caeltia also achieved his change. But Art sat on the ground fingering his raiment, and seemed to be lost in a contemplation of the grass beside him.

Finaun was ready. He stood upright, a kingly figure, shimmering in purple folds. On his head a great crown, closed at the top; across his shoulder a chain of heavy gold, and depending on his breast a broad plaque of gold that blazed.

He looked at the others and nodded, then he leaped, and at a hundred feet the sun flashed from his wings, and he looked like a part of the rainbow.

Now Caeltia was ready, standing in cloth of gold and lovely ornaments of hammered silver. He scanned once more the drowsing landscape; he smiled on Art; he sprang aloft and abroad and sped upwards in a blinding gleam.

Art raised himself.

He lifted the crimson robe that was dashed with gold, the crimson buskins feathered at the heel, the wide crown of short points. He placed these on the ground and stood for a time looking down the road, while the many-coloured pinions streamed lengthily from his hand.

Suddenly he frowned, and, with the wings still dragging, he ran down the path.

In five minutes he came to the place where they had left the ass, but it was no longer there. Far below on the curving ways he saw the donkey moving quietly. Mac Cann and Eileen Ni Cooley were going by each other's side, and Patsy's arm was about the woman.

He looked around, and at a little distance saw the girl beside a bush. She was lying on her breast, her face was hidden into the ground, and she was motionless.

He walked to her.

'Mary,' said he, 'I have come to say farewell.'

She moved as at a shock. She rose to her feet, and she did not look at him, and this was the first time that these two had talked together.

He bent to her beseechingly:

'I have come to say farewell,' said he.

Again she put her hand into his:

'Say your say,' quoth she, 'and go your road,' and with that she did look at him, sternly.

He loosed her hand; his eyes flamed; he stamped the road; he swung his arms aloft gripping the wings, and, with a fierce movement, he ripped them in twain; he put the halves together and tore again, then, with a sweep of his hands, fluttered the shining plumes away and on the wind.

190

'Now!' quoth he, with a laugh.

'Oh!' she stammered, staring, terrified, incredulous.

'Let you and I go down after the people,' he said.

But Mary was weeping, and as they paced down the narrow track he laid a great arm about her shoulder.